Liturgy 101

Sacraments and Sacramentals

DANIEL G. VAN SLYKE

Liguori

Imprimi Potest: Thomas D. Picton, CSsR
Provincial, Denver Province, The Redemptorists

Imprimatur: In accordance with c. 827, permission to publish has been granted on September 21, 2010, by the most Reverend Robert J. Hermann, Vicar General, Archdiocese of Saint Louis. Permission to publish is an indication that nothing contrary to Church teaching is contained in this work. It does not imply any endorsement of the opinions expressed in the publication; nor is any liability assumed by this permission.

Published by Liguori Publications, Liguori, Missouri 63057
To order, call 800-325-9521 or visit Liguori.org

Library of Congress Cataloging-in-Publication Data

Van Slyke, Daniel G.
  Liturgy 101 : sacraments and sacramentals / by Daniel G. Van Slyke.
    p. cm.
  ISBN 978-0-7648-1845-5
  1. Sacraments—Catholic Church. I. Title. II. Title: Liturgy one hundred one.
  BX2200.V36 2010
  264'.0208—dc22

                                                                              2010035553

Scripture selections taken from the *New American Bible with Revised New Testament and Revised Psalms,* copyright © 1991, 1986, 1970 Confraternity of Christian Doctrine, Washington, D.C. 20017, and are used by permission of the copyright owner. All Rights Reserved. No part of the New American Bible may be reproduced in any form without permission in writing from the copyright owner.

Excerpts from copyrighted papal encyclicals, letters, instructions and other publications of the *Libreria Editrice Vaticana* are used with permission.

Excerpts from the English translation of Vatican II constitutions are from *The Documents of Vatican II,* Walter M. Abbott, SJ, ed., (New York: America Press, 1966).

English translation of the *Catechism of the Catholic Church* for the United States of America copyright © 1994, United States Catholic Conference, Inc.—Libreria Editrice Vaticana. English translation of the *Catechism of the Catholic Church: Modifications from the Editio Typica* copyright © 1997, United States Catholic Conference, Inc.—Libreria Editrice Vaticana.

Excerpt from the English translation of *Rite of Baptism for Children* © 1969, International Committee on English in the Liturgy, Inc. (ICEL); excerpt from the English translation of *The Liturgy of the Hours* © 1974, ICEL; excerpts from the English translation of *The Roman Missal* © 2010, ICEL; excerpts from the English translation of *Rite of Penance* © 1974, ICEL; excerpts from the English translation of *Rite of Confirmation (Second Edition)* © 1975, ICEL; excerpts from the English translation of *The Ordination of Deacons, Priests, and Bishops* © 1975, ICEL; excerpts from the English translation of *Pastoral Care of the Sick: Rites of Anointing and Viaticum* © 1982,ICEL. All rights reserved. Used with permission.

Cover design: Jodi Hendrickson
Cover image: Jupiter Images

Printed in the United States of America
22 21 20 19 18   6 5 4 3 2

Contents

Foreword   5

CHAPTER 1 • Words About Worship   7

CHAPTER 2 • Baptism   23

CHAPTER 3 • Confirmation   40

CHAPTER 4 • The Most Holy Sacrament   54

CHAPTER 5 • The Sacrament of Penance   79

CHAPTER 6 • Anointing of the Sick   95

CHAPTER 7 • Holy Orders   105

CHAPTER 8 • Matrimony   123

Conclusion   141

Foreword

Very little, if anything, in this book is original. That is not to say that I do not have original thoughts. I do, and some of them have been published elsewhere. The purpose of this book, however, is not to present my own thoughts or opinions. The purpose is to introduce interested readers to the teachings of the Catholic Church about liturgy—and, more specifically, about the seven sacraments. By the grace of God, my opinions are in alignment with the faith of the Church as articulated by the magisterium, as well as by many holy saints and doctors. My hope is that the reader will come to know better, appreciate more deeply, and love more fervently the gifts that God gives in the seven sacraments.

This book presents the basics of Catholic teachings about the sacraments. I highly recommend that readers pursue additional self-formation in the sacraments using the sources listed in the "further reading" section following each of the chapters. These sources include the Bible, documents written by popes, councils, and various congregations of the Roman Curia, as well as the official liturgical rites of the Catholic Church. Nearly all of these sources are available on the Internet. With the posting of official Church documents on the Internet, those interested in exploring the Catholic faith and its teachings can immediately access many once difficult-to-obtain sources. In each chapter, I have abbreviated names of the sources cited; the abbreviations are spelled out at the end of the chapter.

Over the past decade, I have taught classes on liturgy and the sacraments to undergraduate and graduate students, adults seeking continuing education, permanent diaconate candidates, and seminarians. These students have been enrolled in programs offered through Ave Maria College, The Institute for Pastoral Theology, the Paul VI Pontifical Institute for Catechetical and Pastoral Studies, the Diocese of Tulsa, Mundelein Seminary, and Kenrick-Glennon Seminary. For these students, I developed the teaching materials that provided the foundation for this book.

My dear wife, Laura, has unflaggingly encouraged me to write this book. I also thank my mother-in-law, Sarah Jane. Her visits—alas, all too brief—and assistance with our six children afforded me crucial time to complete this manuscript. She also read several of the chapters and helped me clarify a number of passages.

My sincerest gratitude goes to colleagues and friends who have read and commented on this book. Edward N. Peters helped me improve the text by carefully reviewing and rigorously commenting on most of the manuscript. Samuel F. Weber, OSB, read through the entire manuscript and offered a number of helpful recommendations. James Baur provided encouraging feedback on drafts of several chapters. C. Eugene Morris provided comments on the first two chapters; Kristian Teater reviewed drafts of four chapters; Edward Richard reviewed the chapter on penance; Robert Fastiggi, the chapter on holy orders; and John Gresham, the chapter on matrimony.

Father John J. Steger died in 2008 after 55 years of tirelessly serving as a parish priest in upstate New York. He baptized hundreds of babies and administered first penance and holy Communion to countless children, including the author of this book. Through the powerful example of Father Steger's selfless, long-suffering perseverance, the Lord has kept me on the path of faith that has brought me to the moment that I write these words of dedication. May the almighty Lord grant him *locum refrigerii, lucis et pacis*—an abode of refreshment, light, and peace.

AT SAINT LOUIS, ON THE FEAST OF SAINT BASIL THE GREAT, 2010
GLORY BE TO THE FATHER, AND TO THE SON, AND TO THE HOLY SPIRIT

CHAPTER 1

Words About Worship

Because words such as "liturgy" and "sacrament" mean different things in different contexts, a brief explanation of the fundamental terms and concepts is helpful before addressing the Church's theology and practice of liturgy and the sacraments. This first chapter sets forth the basic understandings of several key terms that will appear in subsequent chapters: liturgy, sacrament, participation, Rite (with an uppercase "R"), rite (lowercase "r"), ordinary, and extraordinary.

LITURGY

Liturgy started its long career as a term for worship in the pages of sacred Scripture. In the ancient Greek version of the Old Testament—known as the *Septuagint*—the words from which liturgy is derived (the verb *leitourgein* and the noun *leitourgia*) occur roughly one hundred times. Liturgy emerges as a technical term for the service or ministry performed by priests in ancient Israel when they offered sacrifices to the Lord. In the New Testament, the Greek word for liturgy continues to designate the priest's ministry (Luke 1:23). The term is especially important to the author of Hebrews, who writes that a priest of the old covenant is constantly engaged in the liturgy, "offering frequently those same sacrifices that can never take away sins" (Hebrews 10:11).

By contrast, Christ the High Priest of the new covenant performs a more excellent liturgy (Hebrews 8:6). Christ offers the one single sacrifice of his own blood on the cross, by which "he has made perfect forever those who are being consecrated" (Hebrews 10:14; see also 9:14). In light of these passages from the New Testament, early Greek-speaking Christians naturally used the word "liturgy" to indicate the offering of the one sacrifice of Christ in the Eucharist at the hands of ordained Christian priests. The term "liturgy" also has a broader but related meaning in several other New Testament passages. In some instances, it is used to designate a general spiritual service performed by faithful Christians—either a service of worship (Acts 13:2) or of charity (Romans 15:27; 2 Corinthians 9:12).

The Christian tradition also employs more general words to describe divine worship. From ancient times, Greek Christians used the word *latria* to indicate the worship that is due to God alone. In fact, *latria* survives as a technical term for "the adoration given to God alone" in Catholic catechesis to this day *(CCCC 286)*. Saint Augustine of Hippo (d. 430) noted that *latria* is usually translated into Latin as service *(servitus)*, although no Latin term conveyed the meaning of the Greek word *latria*. Other possible contenders he discussed include cult *(cultus)*, religion *(religio)*, and piety *(pietas)*, but none of these has the precise meaning of *latria*.

In the Middle Ages, Latin authors described what would today be called liturgy with such words as duty *(munus)*, ministry *(ministerium)*, service *(servitus)*, office *(officium)*, and cult *(cultus)*. A book about the liturgy would have been titled A Treatise on the Offices in past centuries. "Cult" still appears today in the Latin title of the Congregation for Divine Worship and the Discipline of the Sacraments—which might more literally be called the Congregation for

Divine Cult *(de culto divino)*. The Congregation for Divine Worship (CDW) is the dicastery or office of the Roman Curia, which still teaches and legislates in the area of Catholic liturgy. One can readily understand why the Church avoids using the English word cult in the dicastery's title. It has negative connotations, evoking images of secretive religious groups engaged in strange or subversive activities. By contrast, Christian worship is a public affair.

The Catholic Church began to employ the word liturgy on a regular basis in the twentieth century. Drawing from the rich biblical tradition discussed above, Pope Pius XII in 1947 defined sacred liturgy in his splendid encyclical on the topic, titled *Mediator Dei,* as follows:

> [T]he public worship which our Redeemer as Head of the Church renders to the Father, as well as the worship which the community of the faithful renders to its Founder, and through Him to the heavenly Father. It is, in short, the worship rendered by the Mystical Body of Christ in the entirety of its Head and members. (MD 20)

Elsewhere in the encyclical, Pope Pius XII pinpoints the passion and death of Christ the Redeemer on the cross as the key moment of this worship. On the cross, Christ is the priest who offers the sacrifice, as well as the sacrificial victim who is offered. The entire Church, the entire body of Christ, is involved in this self-offering: Christ as the head of the body, and the faithful as members.

Pope Pius XII's practical understanding of liturgy is rather broad. In his encyclical on the sacred liturgy, he addresses the following topics: the sacraments (first and foremost, the Eucharist), worship of the Eucharist, personal preparation for celebrating the sacraments, and the Divine Office or Liturgy of the Hours. Closely related topics the pope also considers include the yearly cycle of feasts of the Lord and feasts of the saints, personal piety, Church decoration, and Gregorian chant.

SACRAMENT: FROM BIBLICAL ROOTS TO A DEVELOPED DEFINITION

As discussed above, "liturgy" originates from a Greek word. "Sacrament," on the other hand, originates from the Latin word *sacramentum*. Sacrament had no exact Greek equivalent. In the Roman Empire at the time that Christianity emerged, "sacrament" indicated the oath of loyalty unto death that Roman soldiers swore to the emperor and one another. The earliest Latin-speaking Christians soon adapted this powerful word, infusing it with their own meaning.

This development of Christian Latin vocabulary occurs in the earliest Latin translations of the Bible—especially in the version known as the Vulgate. The Vulgate is the standard Latin edition of Scripture that has been used in the Western Church since the fifth century. The Vulgate employs the word "sacrament" on fifteen occasions—six of which appear in the books of Daniel and Revelation (Daniel 2:18; 2:30; 2:47; 4:6; Revelation 1:20; 17:7). These apocalyptic books depict visions wherein the seers Daniel and John symbolically witness events that will take place at the end of time. The sacrament in each of these passages is some hidden mystery that is revealed to the seer in a way that does not necessarily make it clearer: through signs and symbols. Examples of this include the giant statue in Nebuchadnezzar's dream, and the seven stars and seven candles in John's visions.

Two elements tie these notions of sacrament together. First, something is being revealed about the divine plan concerning world-shattering events; second, the manner in which that something is revealed is not obvious, but requires interpretation. From ancient Latin versions of the Bible, sacrament emerges as a sign of God's plan that is made manifest and given meaning in Christ—all the while maintaining a hidden or mysterious character.

From the late second century, Latin Christians applied the term sacrament to the most significant liturgical celebrations of the

Church, such as baptism and the Eucharist. Greek-speaking Christians designate these same celebrations as "mysteries." The word also continued to be used in a broader sense to indicate the mysteries of God's revelation in general. This book is concerned with the more specific definition of sacrament that develops with the guidance of the Holy Spirit within the Christian tradition. This definition is the fruit of believers' efforts to understand the mysterious content and the effect of seven central rites of worship.

Following centuries of theological reflection, the elements of a more precise definition of sacrament emerged in the works of such luminaries as Hugh of Saint Victor (d. 1141) and Saint Bernard of Clairvaux (d. 1153). The popular Roman Catechism of the sixteenth century concisely expressed this meaning with words that remain clear and useful to this day: "A Sacrament is a visible sign of an invisible grace, instituted for our justification." Each element of this definition must be examined in order to better understand what a sacrament is and what it does.

INSTITUTED: DIVINE INITIATIVES

"Wisdom has built her house, she has set up her seven columns" (Proverbs 9:1). The fathers and doctors of the Church always have recognized "Wisdom" as the Son of God, who became incarnate as Jesus Christ, the Son of Mary. The house that Christ has built is the Church, and the seven pillars that sustain the house are the sacraments.

Why God endows the number seven with such significance is a mystery, but the number's importance is evident throughout Scripture. God creates the world in six days, and rests on the seventh. The Christian is re-created and sustained by God's grace through the six sacraments, and the seventh prepares for the journey to eternal rest in heaven. When the Flood destroyed the sinful inhabitants of the earth, God saved Noah and seven other people (2 Peter 2:5) on the ark, along with seven pairs of every clean animal. Christians—whose sins are destroyed in the waters of baptism—are saved by the seven sacraments of Christ and the Church. The Church, as the ark or bark of Peter, carries the faithful through the storms of the worldly tribulations and temptations to the safe port of her heavenly homeland.

The ancient Israelites observed seven annual feasts for seven days each, and they also celebrated weddings for seven days (Judges 14:17). It took Solomon seven years to build the Temple of the Lord in Jerusalem (1 Kings 6:38). Turning to the New Testament, after Jesus feeds four thousand men with seven loaves and a few fish, seven baskets of fragments remain (Matthew 15:34–38). Christians have commonly seen these loaves and fish as symbols of the sacraments, beginning with the first appearance of Christian art in the Roman catacombs.

The number seven continues to enjoy preeminence in the worship of the new covenant through the seven sacraments. Like the feasts of the Old Testament, the seven sacraments of the New Testament are divinely instituted—that is, God established them, determined their essential shape, and endowed them with power. Whereas God instituted the worship of the Old Testament or the Old Law through Moses (John 1:17; 7:19), our Lord Jesus Christ himself instituted the seven sacraments of the New Covenant. Christ established them, determined their essential shape, and endowed them with power through his blood (Luke 22:20; 1 Corinthians 11:25; Hebrews 12:24)—that is, in his sacrifice on the cross.

Finally, Christ entrusted the sacraments to the Church for the sanctification of the faithful "in his blood," to use once again the language of sacred Scripture (Hebrews 13:12; 1 John 1:7; Ephesians 1:7). Therefore Christ, the High Priest of the New Covenant, is both the historical source of the Church's sacraments and the source of their power, which derives from his passion, death, and resurrection. Not invented or discovered by human beings, the sacraments make sense only as an integral part of God's plan for saving humanity through Christ.

The sacraments belong to the Church in a twofold manner. First, the sacraments are for the Church insofar as they bring the Church into existence and sanctify her members. Second, the sacraments are by the Church insofar as Christ chooses, with the power of the Holy Spirit, to work through the Church to make the sacraments effective. The Church, in turn, expresses faith in Christ through the sacraments. Yet the sacraments are not merely expressions of faith that presuppose faith; they also nourish and strengthen faith (*CCC* 1123).

Therefore when considering any sacrament, the first question to ask is how Christ instituted it and entrusted it to the Church. The chapters of this book will address the scriptural foundations of each sacrament, as established by Christ.

A Visible Sign: The Essential Rite

The next central concept regarding any sacrament is its essential rite. Each of the seven sacraments is marked by an essential rite, without which the sacrament cannot exist. The essential rite is a tangible sign—it can be experienced through one or more of the five senses. It can be heard, seen, felt, smelled, or tasted. The essential rite includes four exterior elements: matter, form, minister, and recipient.

The matter of a sacrament includes both a physical or sensorial element, as well as the action with which it is applied. For example, in baptism the physical element is water. Yet water sitting in a font does not make a sacrament. The water must be applied to a catechumen or an infant who is presented for baptism. Furthermore, the purpose of the application of the physical object must be specified by the form or verbal formula. In the case of baptism, the form is: "I baptize you in the name of the Father, and of the Son, and of the Holy Spirit." By contrast, if a mother pours water on her baby three times saying, "I am going to get that applesauce off you," no sacrament takes place. The form determines the purpose of the use of the physical element. Therefore the form also is part of the essential rite.

The proper minister and recipient also are necessary elements of each sacrament. For a sacrament to be valid, both the minister and the recipient must be live human beings. Fido the dog can neither baptize, nor can he be baptized. An angel cannot administer, nor can a corpse receive, any sacrament. When celebrating a sacrament, the minister must intend to do what the Church does in that sacrament. This is not the same as intending to do what the Church intends. To intend, or fully understand, the mystery of a sacrament is not required on the part of a given minister. Only ordained bishops and priests can minister the sacraments of confirmation, the Eucharist, penance or reconciliation, anointing of the sick, and holy orders. Anyone, however, can administer baptism: this includes deacons, lay people, and even non-Catholics when necessary.

The question of the recipient or beneficiary of a sacrament is similar. Some people cannot receive certain sacraments. For example, someone who already has been baptized cannot be baptized again. Furthermore, someone not yet baptized cannot receive any of the other six sacraments.

The celebration of a sacrament typically includes many words, gestures, and even objects that are not part of the essential rite, as well as people who are neither ministers nor recipients. The essential rite of baptism, for example, is accompanied by readings and prayers, along with the use of objects such as oil, candles, and white garments. Known as sacramentals, these clothe the essential rite with additional dignity, educate those present about the effects of the sacrament, and excite the minds of the faithful to contemplate God's gift of grace through the sacrament. Nonetheless, sacramentals are not absolutely necessary or essential parts of the sacrament. Whereas the essential rite of each sacrament is instituted by Christ, the Church establishes the sacramentals that surround the essential rite. Why? To promote participation, devotion, and reverence on the part of the faithful. Except in cases of urgent necessity, no minister may omit these sacramentals.

All elements of the essential rite of a sacrament must be present in order for the sacrament to be valid. If part of the essential rite is missing, a sacrament is said to be invalid. If a sacrament is celebrated with all its sacramentals as indicated by the Church in the appropriate liturgical books, it is said to be licit or properly celebrated according to the Church's prescriptions. If some of the sacramentals are missing, the celebration may be illicit or not properly conducted, but still valid.

AN INVISIBLE GRACE. . .FOR OUR JUSTIFICATION

Through the tangible sign of a sacrament, Christ always offers an invisible gift of grace. This grace is for the sake of the salvation of the faithful. The ultimate cause of a Christian's justification is the passion, death, resurrection, and ascension of Christ. Since salvation comes only through the passion, the grace of the sacraments draws the Christian near to the cross, enabling each of Christ's faithful to benefit personally from the infinite fruits of Christ's one perfect sacrifice.

Sacraments are valid and offer grace *ex opere operato*, to use a classical phrase of Latin theology. In other words, sacraments operate by the power of the complete sacramental rite. When the necessary matter and form coincide with a minister and recipient who possess sufficient intention, the sacrament is necessarily present and grace is infallibly offered. Catholics may take great comfort in the fact that God offers grace in the sacraments *ex opere operato*, since this kind of efficacy works regardless of the personal piety of a minister. For example, even a priest guilty of mortal sin can validly minister the sacrament of the Eucharist. So Catholics need not worry about the personal state or the piety of a given minister when they approach one of the seven sacraments; the grace of Christ is infallibly offered in the sacrament *ex opere operato.*

Through the sacraments, according to the Council of Trent, "all true justice either begins, or being begun is increased, or being lost is restored" (CT 7). The sanctifying grace of baptism, for example, justifies the new Christian, brings about the forgiveness of sins, and begins the Christian life as a participation in the very life of God. Grace is God's gift of divine life and power. Sanctifying grace, which is necessary for salvation, can be lost through mortal sin. If lost, however, it can be restored through the sacrament of reconciliation. Sanctifying grace is strengthened and preserved through the sacrament of the Eucharist, and through all of the sacraments received after baptism.

FRUITFUL PARTICIPATION

The invisible grace that is infallibly offered *ex opere operato* through the sacraments does not necessarily benefit or bear fruit in each individual recipient. Some people are better disposed to benefit from the grace than others. The Christian who has strong faith, as well as a burning love for God and neighbor, benefits more from any given sacrament than an individual with little faith and love. Furthermore, if a Christian places an *obex* (obstacle of vice or sin) between himself and God, he or she does not benefit from a sacrament at all.

Each Christian's salvation depends upon participation in the one sacrifice of Christ on the cross. The faithful—both ordained and non-ordained—must strive to participate as fully and fruitfully as possible in that sacrifice through the sacraments. As the Second Vatican Council emphasized: "Mother Church earnestly desires that all the faithful should be led to that fully conscious, and actual participation in liturgical celebrations which is demanded by the very nature of the liturgy" (SC 14). Actual participation in the sacraments is sometimes confused with active participation, which focuses on external activity or serving at the liturgy in visible roles. In the context of liturgy however, "the active participation called for by the council must be understood in more substantial terms, on the basis of a greater awareness of the mystery being celebrated and its relationship to daily life" (SCar 52).

Several factors cultivate such living and fruitful participation. Faith and catechesis prepare the way for appreciation of the sacraments and their relation to the one perfect sacrifice in which the High Priest of the New Covenant shed his blood. A life of active prayer and devotion outside liturgical celebrations enables the Christian to more fully participate in the sacraments. An upright moral life in keeping with the commandments of God, and animated above all by love of God and neighbor (1 John 3:22–23) provides the foundation for worshipping God in spirit and in truth. A humble heart that yearns for God's forgiveness and blessing also is a prerequisite for full participation in the sacraments:

> A heart reconciled to God makes genuine participation possible. The faithful need to be reminded that there can be no *actuosa participatio* [actual participation] in the sacred mysteries without an accompanying effort to participate actively in the life of the Church as a whole, including a missionary commitment to bring Christ's love into the life of society. (SCar 55)

Several habits or dispositions, then, foster ever-deepening participation in the sacraments: faith and formation in the faith, an active habit of prayer, an upright moral life marked by love of God and neighbor, and engagement in the Church's mission. The individual Christian, whose spirit is imbued with such dispositions, is personally prepared fully and fruitfully to participate in the sacraments.

RITES, RITES (SMALL "R"), AND RIGHTS

Rite with an uppercase "R" should be distinguished from rite with a lowercase "r." The latter indicates how a particular ceremony is conducted, including both the essential rite and the sacramentals. Examples of the lowercase "rite" include the rite of baptism and the rite of confirmation. The words or verbal formulas (many of the prayers and chants) and instructions for distinct rites are written in liturgical books, which the Church has developed over many centuries. Since ancient times, instructions in liturgical books have been written in red ink so that the celebrant of the rite is able to easily distinguish them from the prayers and formulae that he reads aloud. These instructions are known as rubrics, from the Latin word *ruber*, which means "red." Each liturgical tradition has its own rites, with its own rubrics and prayer formulas.

The word "Rite" with an uppercase "R" indicates an ancient and broad pattern of liturgical tradition belonging to an ethnic, linguistic, or cultural group. The Byzantine Rite, for example, refers to the liturgical services of Byzantium or Constantinople (known today as Istanbul). These services have been conducted in the Greek language since the fourth century. The Latin Rite emerged from Greek origins in the third and fourth centuries, when Western Christians began worshipping in the Latin tongue.

In the West, various churches had their own Latin Rite liturgies, including the Gallican churches of the Frankish lands (modern-day France and Germany). The influence of the liturgy of Rome, known as Roman Rite, gradually overshadowed other Latin Rite liturgical families. The episcopal See itself and the liturgy of Rome were established by the apostles Peter and Paul. Thus Rome's influence spread because the city boasted the only Apostolic See or bishropic founded by an apostle in the Latin-speaking western half of Europe.

Nonetheless, the Roman Rite itself was enriched throughout the medieval period by contact with other Rites, including the Gallican liturgies. The Roman Rite became even more influential after the printing press was invented in the fifteenth century, and after Roman liturgical books were revised following the Council of Trent in the sixteenth century. Since the earliest publishers wanted to sell liturgical books with the broadest appeal, the Roman Rite was the natural choice.

Today, the Roman Rite is the primary liturgical Rite experienced by Catholics in North America, Europe, Central America, South America, and all over the world. Therefore our focus will be on the rites of the Roman Rite.

As a final consideration, what are the rights of the faithful with regard to liturgy and the sacraments? The Catholic faithful have a right to the rites of the Roman Rite, but nobody has a right to the grace of the sacraments.

No one has a right to the grace of the sacraments because grace is a free gift from God. We can pray for grace, strive to make ourselves worthy of the sacraments, and give God thanks and praise for the gifts he gives in the sacraments. But we cannot earn or demand the grace of God. Therefore we must approach the sacraments with humility if we are to fruitfully participate in them.

Yet the Catholic faithful do have a right to the rites of the Roman Rite. As the Congregation for Divine Worship and the Discipline of the Sacraments has insisted, "it is the right of all of Christ's faithful that the Liturgy, and in particular the celebration of Holy Mass, should truly be as the Church wishes, according to her stipulations as prescribed in the liturgical books and in the other laws and norms" (RS 12). The ministers of the Catholic Church owe to the faithful a dignified celebration of the rites of the sacraments as they are set forth in the liturgical books of the Roman Rite. This right of the faithful and duty of the Church's ministers protects both ministers and recipients of the sacraments from their own cultural limitations and from the whims of influential local personalities. The right of the faithful to the rites of the Church also ensures Christians' access to divine worship in accordance with the mind of the Church and her traditions.

ORDINARY AND EXTRAORDINARY FORMS OF THE ROMAN RITE

In his apostolic letter, *Summorum Pontificum* of July 7, 2007, Pope Benedict XVI explains that there are "two usages of the one Roman rite" (SP article 1). The extraordinary use or form is expressed in the Roman missal first promulgated by Pope Saint Pius V in 1570, the missal reissued in its latest form by Blessed John XXIII in 1962, and in other Roman liturgical books in use immediately before the Second Vatican Council. The ordinary form is found in the Roman missal first promulgated by Pope Paul VI in 1970 and in the other revised liturgical books or rites published following the Second Vatican Council. The most characteristic distinction between these two uses is that the extraordinary form is offered in Latin, whereas the ordinary form is most frequently celebrated in a vernacular language. This difference, however, is only superficial; the ordinary form can also be celebrated in Latin. Nonetheless, the extraordinary form of the Mass is most often referred to as "the traditional Latin Mass" or "the Latin Mass."

The extraordinary form of the Roman Rite is sometimes called "Tridentine," in reference to the Council of Trent (1545–1563). This appellation is not entirely correct: the rites of the extraordinary form, or significant parts of them, predate the Council of Trent. These liturgical books also were emended on several occasions following the Council of Trent.

In this case, the Church appears to use the technical term extraordinary to indicate something that adds to, or complements, the ordinary. In a similar use of the term, an extraordinary session of a synod of bishops may complement the work of the ordinary session.

By generously allowing celebration of the extraordinary form of the Roman Rite, Pope Benedict XVI indicates that the two usages complement one another. Together, they enrich the beauty and depth of divine worship in the unity of the one Church.

Some observers object to the pope's generosity toward the extraordinary form, arguing that it promotes division among the faithful. On the contrary, the Church has always known and allowed a variety of Rites and uses, and has never enforced absolute liturgical uniformity. Legitimate liturgical diversity is a feature of the one universal Church, and it illustrates an important theological point: "The mystery of Christ is so unfathomably rich that it cannot be exhausted by its expression in any single liturgical tradition" (*CCC* 1201).

DISCUSSION QUESTIONS

1. *Which book of the Bible most explicitly discusses the liturgy of Christ the High Priest? How does that book shed light on the Church's worship?*

2. *What have the Greek and Latin languages contributed to the vocabulary that the Church uses to discuss liturgy?*

3. *In light of biblical evidence for the meaning of the term liturgy, how might the oft-repeated definition as "work of the people" be misleading?*

4. *Provide a basic definition of the term sacrament.*

5. *What factors foster actual participation in the sacraments?*

ABBREVIATIONS AND SOURCES

CCC: *Catechism of the Catholic Church*. 2nd ed. Washington, D.C.: United States Catholic Conference, 1994, 1997.

CCCC: *Compendium of the Catechism of the Catholic Church*. Washington, D.C.: United States Conference of Catholic Bishops, 2006.

CT 7: Council of Trent, Session 7. Decree and Canons on the Sacraments in General. March 3, 1547.

MD: Pope Pius XII. Encyclical on the Sacred Liturgy *Mediator Dei*. November 20, 1947.

RS: Congregation for Divine Worship and the Discipline of the Sacraments. Instruction on Certain Matters to be Observed or to be Avoided Regarding the Most Holy Eucharist *Redemptionis Sacramentum*. March 25, 2004. © 2004 Libreria Editrice Vaticana.

SC: Second Vatican Council. Constitution on the Liturgy *Sacrosanctum Concilium*. December 4, 1963.

SCar: Pope Benedict XVI. Post-Synodal Apostolic Exhortation on the Eucharist as the Source and Summit of the Church's Life and Mission *Sacramentum Caritatis*. February 22, 2007. © 2007 Libreria Editrice Vaticana.

SP: Pope Benedict XVI. Apostolic Letter Given Motu Proprio *Summorum Pontificum*. July 7, 2007. © 2007 Libreria Editrice Vaticana.

FOR FURTHER READING

Arinze, Francis; George, Francis; Medina, Jorge; and Pell, George. *Cardinal Reflections: Active Participation and the Liturgy*. Chicago: Hillenbrand Books, 2005.

Hahn, Scott. *Swear to God: The Promise and Power of the Sacraments*. New York: Doubleday Religion, 2004.

Ratzinger, Joseph. *The Spirit of the Liturgy*. Trans. John Saward. San Francisco: Ignatius Press, 2000.

CHAPTER 2

Baptism

The Gateway to Sacramental Life

This chapter explores how the sacrament of baptism is "a visible sign of an invisible grace, instituted for our justification." First, we will discuss the divine initiative whereby Christ institutes baptism as the sacrament of spiritual birth. The invisible grace or effect of baptism provides the next topic for investigation. Then the visible sign or essential rite will be set forth, including the matter, form, minister, and recipient. Subsequent sections about the baptism of infants and adults will examine in more detail the recipients of baptism, as well as the liturgical contexts in which they receive the sacrament. The final section is devoted to practical questions regarding godparents and secret baptisms.

SPIRITUAL BIRTH AND DIVINE INSTITUTION

From the moment of creation, water is featured as an element of birth and new life (see Genesis 1:1–2). The waters in the womb of a mother provide the protective environment in which each infant develops, the environment in which God himself forms the individual (Isaiah 49:1, 5; Jeremiah 1:5). At the moment of the Incarnation,

Christ is conceived in the womb of the Blessed Virgin Mary by the power of the Holy Spirit (Luke 1:31, 35). As God becomes man in the waters of Mary's womb, so each Christian is reborn by the power of the Holy Spirit in the waters of the Church's womb, the baptismal font.

"At this font," the inscription in the baptistery of Saint John Lateran reads, "the Church, our mother, gives birth from her virginal womb to the children she conceived by the power of the Holy Spirit." Such imagery is already found in sacred Scripture. Christ explains to Nicodemus that "no one can see the kingdom of God without being born from above" (John 3:3). Nicodemus misunderstands: "How can a person once grown old be born again? Surely he cannot reenter his mother's womb and be born again, can he?" (John 3:4). Jesus responds, "no one can enter the kingdom of God without being born of water and Spirit" (John 3:5). With these words, Christ reveals the mystery of the mission with which he will entrust the Church after his resurrection: "Go, therefore, and make disciples of all nations, baptizing them in the name of the Father, and of the Son, and of the Holy Spirit, teaching them to observe all that I have commanded you" (Matthew 28:19–20). With this post-resurrection command to his followers, the risen Lord institutes the sacrament of baptism.

Going back in time to the beginning of Jesus' ministry on earth, John the Baptist baptized Christ "to fulfill all righteousness" (Matthew 3:15). As John immediately recognized, Christ had no need of baptism for the forgiveness of sin. By submitting to John's baptism, the Lord gave the waters of earth the power of sanctifying, set an example for his followers, and revealed the work of the most holy Trinity as the Holy Spirit descended in the form of a dove, and the voice of the Father resounded from above (Matthew 3:16–17; Mark 1:10–11; Luke 3:22).

DEATH TO SIN AND NEW LIFE IN THE TRINITY: THE INVISIBLE GRACE

The apostles began to fulfill Christ's charge to baptize the nations on the day of Pentecost. On that day, Saint Peter concluded the first sermon ever delivered by a Christian with an exhortation: "Repent and be baptized, every one of you, in the name of Jesus Christ for the forgiveness of your sins" (Acts 2:38). Three thousand people heeded Peter's words and received baptism the same day (Acts 2:41).

It is no coincidence that Peter interprets the Flood as a figure or prophecy of Christian baptism (1 Peter 3:20–21). The Flood cleansed the earth of the wickedness of sin, and humanity received a fresh start through Noah. In the same way, baptism cleanses the individual from original sin as well as sins personally committed, imparting a fresh start to the new life of grace in Christ. This is the first major effect or invisible grace of the sacrament: purification from sin. God alone can forgive sins (Mark 2:7), and the forgiveness of sins comes to the world through the passion of Christ: "In him we have redemption by his blood, the forgiveness of transgressions, in accord with the riches of his grace" (Ephesians 1:7).

Baptism effects the forgiveness of sins specifically because through baptism God applies to an individual the fruits of Christ's crucifixion and death: "we who were baptized into Christ Jesus were baptized into his death" (Romans 6:3). Through the merits of Christ's passion, all sins are forgiven in baptism—original and personal, mortal and venial. Baptism also frees an individual from temporal and eternal punishments owed for sin. The eternal punishment is damnation or hell. Freed from sin and justified by the sanctifying grace of baptism, the Christian is prepared for the eternal bliss of heaven. One whom God sustains in sanctifying grace is said to be in a "state of grace."

The temporal penalty owed for sin includes the penalty one must pay, or the amends one must make, for sins that God has forgiven.

This penalty is temporal because it has an end; it will not last forever. Since baptism erases the temporal punishment owed for sin, the new Christian need not complete his baptism with any penance, as is required of the recipient of the sacrament of reconciliation. Nonetheless, a certain tendency or inclination toward sin remains even in the baptized. Catholic tradition calls this tendency concupiscence, and firmly distinguishes concupiscence from sin properly speaking (CT 5). The newly baptized are completely cleansed from sin, but they must struggle with concupiscence even as they progress by God's grace along the path of spiritual growth. Thus the first effect of baptism—forgiveness of sins—is the necessary foundation for the sacrament's second effect, which is birth to the Christian spiritual life.

As Saint Paul explains, dying to sin with Christ in baptism enables the Christian to rise with Christ in the new life of his resurrection: "We were indeed buried with him through baptism into death, so that, just as Christ was raised from the dead by the glory of the Father, we too might live in newness of life" (Romans 6:4). The new life in sanctifying grace or the state of grace, the Christian life itself, begins with baptism. Indeed, this life in Christ is only possible through the forgiveness of sins, which baptism accomplishes. Where sin and death come to an end, Christian life begins in the waters of baptism. "Whoever hears my word and believes in the one who sent me has eternal life and will not come to condemnation, but has passed from death to life" (John 5:24).

This is the life of justification, the life lived in sanctifying grace. "I came," says Christ, "so that they might have life and have it more abundantly" (John 10:10). Such is the second major category of the invisible grace of baptism: abundant, even eternal life in the Father, the Son, and the Holy Spirit—participation through grace in the very life of the triune God.

New birth in the baptismal font, the virginal womb of the

Church, brings the Christian into a new family, that of the baptized. Baptism in the passion of Christ is the foundation of the Church, the means by which one becomes a member of the Church. Through baptism one becomes a Christian, incorporated into the Church, the body of Christ: "For in one Spirit we were all baptized into one body, whether Jews or Greeks, slaves or free persons, and we were all given to drink of one Spirit" (1 Corinthians 12:13). Thus the Creed recited at Mass immediately connects the Church with baptism: "I believe in one, holy, catholic and apostolic Church. I confess one baptism for the forgiveness of sins."

In the above paragraphs, we have explored baptism's twofold invisible grace or effect: forgiveness of sin, and new life in Christ and the Church. A third effect of the sacrament, the character or enduring mark that baptism imprints on the soul, will be addressed in the final section of this chapter. In the meantime, we will investigate the visible sign of baptism, including the essential rite, and the liturgical contexts in which the sacrament is administered.

THE VISIBLE SIGN OF BAPTISM

The Christian spiritual life and membership in the Church begin with the simple but necessary matter or element of water. In fact, baptism draws its very name from water: the Greek word *baptizein* means "to plunge" or "to immerse." The matter of baptism is immersion into water or a pouring of water on the recipient. The water must be applied three times while the form or formula is proclaimed. The baptismal formula has remained consistent throughout history in two variations. (For the sake of following this discussion, you may want to review the final two sections of the first chapter: "Rites, rites, and Rights" and "Ordinary and Extraordinary Forms of the Roman Rite.")

The first variation, found both in the ordinary and the extraordinary form of the Roman Rite, attributes a more active role to the human minister: "N., I baptize you in the name of the Father, and of the Son, and of the Holy Spirit." The second variation, in use among most Eastern Rites, is a passive construction: "The servant of God N. is baptized in the name of the Father, and of the Son, and of the Holy Spirit." The "N." in this construction is the name of the *baptizandus*, or the one to be baptized. Both variations of the baptismal form derive from the resurrected Lord's words of institution (Matthew 28:20), and both clearly demonstrate that the sacrament's power directly derives from the triune God.

The minister must pronounce the form while performing the immersion or pouring of water upon the recipient. Who is the minister of this sacrament? The ordinary ministers of baptism are those in holy orders: bishops, priests, and deacons. In cases of necessity, however, any human being who intends to do what the Church does and who uses the proper matter and form can validly baptize—even someone who is not a Christian. In other words, under extreme circumstances such as the absence of ordained clergy or instances in which death appears imminent, anyone can baptize.

This radical latitude in the ability to administer baptism stems from the saving will of God, "who wills everyone to be saved and to come to knowledge of the truth" (1 Timothy 2:4). Christ reveals the necessity of baptism for salvation when he tells Nicodemus that "no one can enter the kingdom of God without being born of water and Spirit" (John 3:5). Moreover, God has revealed to the Church no means other than baptism by which anyone can be assured salvation. "Whoever believes and is baptized will be saved; whoever does not believe will be condemned" (Mark 16:16).

Two oft-heard phrases immediately arise in this connection: baptism by blood and baptism by desire. In both cases, God grants the saving grace of baptism without the essential rite of ablution with water. Baptism by blood takes place when, strictly speaking, someone is martyred for faith in Christ before being baptized. The second category of non-water baptism is baptism by desire. This describes the case of a catechumen who is preparing for baptism but dies before receiving the sacrament. In both baptism by blood and baptism by desire, baptism, charity, and repentance for sins accompany an explicit desire to be baptized.

Since charity, repentance, and desire for baptism can be found only in one who has reached the age of reason, infants who have died without baptism, including aborted fetuses, do not fall into the category of those saved through baptism by desire or by blood. God has not revealed the fate of such infants to the Church, which

> ...can only entrust them to the mercy of God.... Indeed, the great mercy of God who desires that all men should be saved, and Jesus' tenderness toward children which caused him to say: 'Let the children come to me, do not hinder them,' [Mark 10: 14; see also 1 Timothy 2:4] allow us to hope that there is a way of salvation for children who have died without Baptism (*CCC* 1261).

This hope is expressed in the funeral rites for children who die without baptism. In various dioceses, this hope also is found in memorial services for the naming of infants who have died before birth or before baptism.

BAPTIZING BABIES

In light of the necessity of baptism for salvation and the Church's desire to fulfill the command and will of Christ, the call to bring infants to the saving sacrament is urgent. Regardless of age, any living human being who has not been baptized is eligible for baptism. Since the time of the apostles, loving parents who want what is best for their children—eternal life in Christ—have brought their babies to the Church's ministers for baptism. Babies benefit from the two main effects granted in baptism. First, they are baptized for the forgiveness of sin—in this case, the original sin inherited from their parents rather than actual sin personally committed (CT 5). Second, infants are brought through baptism into the life of the Holy Trinity, incorporated into the Body of Christ as members of the Church. Thus baptized children inherit the dignity of children of God.

The baptism of infants illustrates two fundamental truths regarding the sacraments and God's plan for salvation. First, no one deserves the grace of salvation, which God gratuitously grants as a sheer unmerited gift. The infant has done nothing to deserve God's love and favor and eternal life; yet Christ grants this grace through baptism. Second, the Christian is called to grow in faith and in the life of faith, the Christian moral life, even after baptism. No Catholic should be so foolish as to proclaim that baptism alone ensures salvation. The Christian who has reached the age of reason must also possess the divine gift of faith and exercise love or charity in order to enter into the kingdom of God.

The baptism of infants, then, serves as a warning to adults who are tempted to be lukewarm toward the Christian moral life. All must strive to grow in the Christian life begun at baptism, through ongoing formation in the faith, devotional fervor, and active charity. Each baptized Christian must pursue that continuous conversion whereby one turns ever more toward Christ. Thus the family and the local church responsible for baptizing an infant, and especially the child's parents and godparents, also are responsible for that child's ongoing formation as a Christian. Incorporation into the Church entails the responsibility to obey God's law, "to observe all that I have commanded you" (Matthew 28:20).

Parents or caregivers, godparents, and the local church form baptized children to follow Christ not only through words of instruction, but also by their example of living in fidelity to the Gospel. Therefore the Church seeks parental consent and some assurance that any infant brought for baptism will be given a Catholic upbringing (instruction on Infant Baptism (PA 15). Baptism without such assurance is valid, but it is not licit. Many well-intentioned older Christians wonder if they may baptize their grandchildren without their parent's knowledge or consent. Such a course of action should not be pursued for a number of reasons. Among those reasons is the fundamental necessity of post-baptismal formation in the faith, without which the child will not benefit from baptism in later years.

Owing to the necessity of baptism for salvation, an infant should be baptized right away if death appears to be imminent. Under less dire circumstances, parents should bring their infants for baptism within a few weeks after birth. The ministers of the Church cannot absolutely deny the request of parents who seek baptism for their infants. Pastors may counsel some delay, however, for the sake of educating parents in the faith and seeking to assure that the baptized child indeed will be raised Catholic. When determining the appropriate time for a baptism, the pastor must take three factors into account: the child's welfare; the state of the parents, who should be present if possible; and various pastoral considerations, including the preparation of parents for the responsibility of forming their child in the faith (BC 8).

Some voices today advocate delaying baptism until children are old enough to decide whether they want to be Christian and whether they want to make a personal commitment to the faith. Our Lord seems to respond to this objection when he admonishes: "Let the children come to me; do not prevent them, for the kingdom of God belongs to such as these" (Mark 10:14). In his mercy, Christ refuses to exclude children from his ministry of salvation. Nor does Jesus exclude infants from his universal command to baptize all nations (Matthew 28:20), which is at the heart of the Church's mission.

Following the Lord's example, the Church from time immemorial has baptized infants. Such Fathers of the Church as Saint Irenaeus of Lyons (who wrote around 180), Saint Cyprian of Carthage (d. 258), and Origen of Alexandria (d. 253), bear witness that the baptism of infants is an apostolic tradition. Saint Augustine of Hippo (d. 430) relates that many parents rushed their infants to church for baptism immediately after birth.

The magisterium of the Church has constantly defended this practice that has been so deeply rooted in the love and the faith of the laity for centuries. The Second Lateran Council of 1139, for example, threatens those who attack infant baptism with excommunication. This demonstrates the seriousness with which the Church has always understood the extension of the Lord's salvation to children, as well as the necessity for baptism, even for infants. Just as God desired to bring infants into the old covenant through circumcision when they were only eight days old (Genesis 17:12), so God in his mercy and love extends the new covenant in Christ's blood to infants through baptism.

OLDER RECIPIENTS OF BAPTISM

Those preparing for baptism after having attained the age of reason should meet several criteria. The first is the desire to be baptized. Baptism must never be forced on anyone. Second, faith is necessary for baptism. Indeed, baptism is the sacrament of faith. As such, baptism is not only a sign of faith, but it also is a cause of faith. In the case of an infant, the faith of the parents or of the Christian community is shared with the child. The faith required for baptism need not be a mature and perfect faith. It is rather a beginning of faith, which the new Christian must nurture and grow with God's help.

Finally, repentance for past sins and a resolution to avoid sinning in the future also is required on the part of the catechumen before baptism. Baptism is the preeminent sacrament of the forgiveness of sins. As discussed above, baptism wipes away not only all sins that the catechumen has ever committed, but also all the punishment owed for those sins. Even so, God grants forgiveness only to those who repent. Therefore the call to baptism is always accompanied by the call to repentance: "Repent and be baptized" (Acts 2:38).

An adult who presents himself or herself for baptism without repentance and sorrow for sin will not benefit from the grace of the sacrament; it will bear no fruit in him. The same observation applies to one who falls into serious and unrepentant sin after baptism—such a Christian will not attain eternal life. Sanctifying grace, the life of the spirit given at baptism, may be lost through the negligence and sin of the one baptized. Chapter five, which is devoted to the sacrament of penance, will address this topic in more detail.

THE CONTEXTS OF BAPTISM

For adults and children who have reached the age of reason, the Church provides a program of Christian initiation by stages or grades called the Rite of Christian Initiation of Adults (RCIA). In 1972, the RCIA was published in response to the mandate of the Second Vatican Council:

> The catechumenate for adults, comprising several distinct steps, is to be restored....By this means the time of the catechumenate, which is intended as a period of suitable instruction, may be sanctified by sacred rites to be celebrated at successive intervals of time. (SC 64)

With these words, the council called for the restoration of the ancient catechumenate as it had developed in the late fourth and early fifth centuries. At that point, large numbers of pagans within the Roman Empire began converting to Christianity. In order to test and prepare them for membership in the Church, pastors submitted these catechumens to a lengthy and rigorous program of preparation. This preparation included extensive instruction in divine revelation, disciplines of fasting and abstinence, and frequent minor exorcisms. The minor or ordinary exorcisms that prepare catechumens for baptism must be distinguished from the major or solemn exorcisms used on those thought to be physically possessed by demons. Minor exorcisms purge catechumens of demonic influences, bringing them out of the kingdom of darkness and into the light of the kingdom of God so that they may become temples of the Holy Spirit (Acts 26:18; Colossians 1:13).

The RCIA is not in itself a catechetical program. Rather, it provides liturgical rites that punctuate the extended time over which individuals prepare for baptism through learning about the faith, getting to know active Christians, engaging in the mission of the Church, and experiencing liturgical worship.

The first liturgical rite of the RCIA is the rite of acceptance, which marks an individual's choice to enter into the catechumenate to learn more about the Catholic faith. The period of the catechumenate may last for many years. During this time, pastors and catechists thoroughly instruct the catechumens in Christian doctrine and morals (RCIA 75–76). The catechumenate also is marked by occasional "celebrations of the word of God," which include scriptural readings, homilies, minor exorcisms, and blessings.

The stage of the catechumenate ends and the period of enlightenment begins with the rite of election or enrollment of names, which typically takes place on the first Sunday of Lent. At this point, catechumens are called the "elect," because they have been chosen by Christ and his Church for baptism at the Easter Vigil. During Mass on the third, fourth, and fifth Sundays of Lent, the catechumens experience the scrutinies. Scrutinies are rites of self-searching and repentance that occur within the Mass, and that include minor exorcisms and public prayers for the elect. The period of enlightenment ends at the Easter Vigil, during which the elect receive the sacraments of initiation—baptism, confirmation, and first holy Communion. The newly baptized then enter into a period of postbaptismal formation in the faith, which is known as "mystagogy."

An adult need not necessarily go through the entire RCIA process in order to be baptized. The rite is highly flexible and can be adapted to a variety of circumstances. Adults in exceptional circumstances, for example, may go through a modified version of the RCIA that takes place in one continuous service, completed in one day. An adult in such an exceptional circumstance might include a soldier who is suddenly deployed to a foreign land. Similarly, someone in danger of death should be baptized without delay. In such a case, all but the essential rites may be omitted as necessary. It is up to the local bishop and the pastor to determine how the RCIA process is conducted in a given diocese or parish, with the primary consideration being the good of the souls of those seeking baptism. Many dioceses have developed handbooks or guidelines for the RCIA process that are distributed by diocesan offices of worship or offices of Catholic education.

In addition to the RCIA, the Church provides an ordinary form Rite of Baptism for Children used when baptizing those who are not yet old enough to receive instruction. If this rite takes place within the celebration of Mass, it follows the homily. Outside of the Mass, the rite still includes a liturgy of the word with scriptural readings and a homily, as well as petitions from the faithful for the infant to be baptized. The celebrant offers a prayer of exorcism, which is followed by anointing with the oil of catechumens. In accordance with a very ancient custom, the waters of the baptismal font are blessed—unless they have recently been blessed at the Easter Vigil. Next, the parents and godparents, on behalf of the child, renounce the devil before professing faith in the holy Trinity.

The essential rite follows the profession of faith. After the actual baptism, three explanatory rites, or sacramentals, emphasize certain effects of baptism. First, an anointing with blessed scented oil called chrism signifies and effects that the new Christian has been baptized into the Body of Christ, the anointed one. Second, the baptized infant is presented with a white garment, which symbolizes the purity or absence of sin in the new Christian soul. Finally, a lighted candle is presented to signify, among other things, the light of Christ that the infant is called to carry into the world following baptism: "if we walk in the light as [God] is in the light, then we have fellowship with one another, and the blood of his Son Jesus cleanses us from all sin" (1 John 1:7).

The extraordinary form of baptism utilizes the same explanatory rites: chrism, a white garment, and a lighted candle. Prayers in the extraordinary form of baptism often emphasize the need for God's help as the newly baptized Christian struggles to live according to the light of baptism. The ordinary-form rite of baptism, on the other hand, generally avoids language depicting Christian life as a battle against evil. The changes in language and the number of minor exorcisms account for the most striking differences between the baptismal rites of the ordinary and of the extraordinary form.

The ordinary form of baptism also assumes that the parents are present for the baptism. In this form, there are several addresses directed toward parents, exhorting them to form the baptized child in the faith. The ordinary form of baptism reflects a change in medical circumstances surrounding childbirth. Due to medical advances in the twentieth century, childbirth is less dangerous for many women, and the recovery time following childbirth is shorter than it used to be. Infant mortality also has declined, and as a result baptism can be delayed for some days or weeks without fear that the infant will die unbaptized. These advances mean that more parents are present for baptisms of infants, and the rite of the ordinary form takes the presence of parents into account.

PRACTICAL QUESTIONS: GODPARENTS AND CLANDESTINE BAPTISMS

Can a non-Christian or a Protestant serve as a godparent at a Catholic baptism? The short answer is "no." Godparents are called to assist their godchildren in living the Gospel both in their personal and social lives, to guide the candidate's progress in the baptismal life, and to sustain their godchildren in moments of hesitancy and anxiety (RCIA 11). In other words, godparents are called to be examples and guides in the Catholic life. Therefore they must be fully initiated Catholics at least sixteen years of age, who have been baptized and confirmed, and who regularly participate in the Eucharist. The parents or the catechumen select the godparents. Each child or catechumen should have at least one godparent. If there are two, one should be male and the other female. A child's mother or father cannot serve as a godparent; nor can anyone who is bound by a canonical penalty such as interdict or excommunication (*CCL* 874).

Can an individual baptize his or her own grandchild, or any other young child? Once again, the answer is "no." Except in cases where there is an immediate danger of death, baptisms should be conducted by those to whom the Church entrusts the task, especially the local pastors. Furthermore, a licit baptism of an infant demands the consent of at least one parent. Not only is consent necessary, but a minister should have a well-grounded hope that the child will be formed as a Catholic. Such a hope can be manifest in one parent's promise that the child will be raised Catholic. The baptism of young children demands post-baptismal catechesis and formation in the faith, lest the child stray from the faith in later years. Raising children Catholic is not the responsibility of parents alone; the entire Christian community is called to share in this responsibility.

Similarly, Catholics must not force an unwilling person to be baptized. One who has reached the age of reason must have manifested an intention to receive baptism, and must have some instruction in and commitment to the doctrines of the faith and the moral life of the Gospel (*CCL* 865).

THE GATEWAY OF THE SHEEPFOLD

"Amen, amen, I say to you, I am the gate for the sheep....Whoever enters through me will be saved, and will come in and go out and find pasture" (John 10:7, 9). The pasture of Christ the Good Shepherd has long been a symbol of paradise. The life of the blessed in heaven begins with the sacrament of baptism on earth. That sacrament, to repeat a fundamental point, enables an individual Christian to benefit from the infinite merits won by Christ in his sacrifice on the cross. Incorporated into the body of Christ through baptism, one enters into the life of grace and becomes a member of the Church, of the Christian faithful. Thus baptism is the door or gateway to the whole Christian life: to adoption as children of God, to membership in the Church, to the eternal bliss of heaven. Baptism also is the gateway to the other sacraments, since it is a prerequisite for validly receiving any of the other six (CCC 1213).

This leads to a final consideration—the indelible spiritual mark that baptism imprints upon the soul. Baptism is the first of the three sacraments that impart such a character—the others are confirmation and holy orders. Since the character is permanent, it is not possible for these sacraments to be received more than once by any individual. Although the invisible grace of forgiveness of sins and new life in Christ can be lost through sin, the character of baptism remains throughout the Christian's life. It constitutes a pledge or seal on the part of God that the Christian who remains steadfast in faith and love will be granted the grace to persevere in Christian life and to enjoy the eternal beatitude of the saints in heaven. Above all, the baptismal character disposes one to worship God and to fruitfully participate in the liturgy.

The sanctifying grace or state of grace effected by baptism, necessary for salvation, may be lost through serious sin. In such instances, that grace can be restored through the sacrament of penance.

Then the never-lost baptismal character once again shines forth, by the mercy of God, and the repentant Christian again benefits from the grace of baptism.

DISCUSSION QUESTIONS

1. *What does sacred Scripture teach about the sacrament of baptism?*

2. *What is the matter and form of the sacrament of baptism?*

3. *What are the effects of the sacrament of baptism?*

4. *Who is the minister of baptism?*

5. *Why baptize babies?*

ABBREVIATIONS AND SOURCES

BC: Rite of Baptism for Children. In *The Rites of the Catholic Church*, vol. 1, pp. 361–466. Collegeville, MN: Liturgical Press, 1990.

CCC: *Catechism of the Catholic Church*, 1213–1284.

CCL: *Code of Canon Law*. Canons 849–878. Latin-English Edition. Trans. Canon Law Society of America. Washington, D.C.: Canon Law Society of America, 1998.

CT 5: Council of Trent, Session 5. Decree Concerning Original Sin. June 17, 1546.

CT 7: Council of Trent, Session 7. Canons on Baptism. March 3, 1547.

PA: Sacred Congregation for the Doctrine of the Faith. Instruction on Infant Baptism *Pastoralis Actio*. 20 October 1980.

SC: Second Vatican Council. Constitution on the Sacred Liturgy *Sacrosanctum Concilium*. December 4, 1963.

FOR FURTHER READING

Lang, David P. *Why Matter Matters: Philosophical and Scriptural Reflections on the Sacraments*. Huntington, IN: Our Sunday Visitor, 2002.

Spinks, Bryan D. *Early and Medieval Rituals and Theologies of Baptism: From the New Testament to the Council of Trent*. Aldershot: Ashgate Publishing Company, 2006

CHAPTER 3

Confirmation
Mission and Power

CHRIST'S MISSION AND THE CHURCH'S MISSION

At the Last Supper, Christ promised his apostles that the Holy Spirit would come to them. "And I will ask the Father, and he will give you another Advocate to be with you always, the Spirit of truth, which the world cannot accept, because it neither sees nor knows it" (John 14:16–17). Having completed his earthly ministry with his passion, death, and resurrection, our Lord reiterated his promise immediately before ascending into heaven: "…you will receive power when the holy Spirit comes upon you, and you will be my witnesses in Jerusalem, throughout Judea and Samaria, and to the ends of the earth" (Acts 1:8).

Just ten days later, on the feast of Pentecost, the Lord fulfilled his promise in a dramatic way. The twelve apostles, along with the Most Blessed Virgin Mary, were praying together in Jerusalem when "a noise like a strong driving wind…filled the entire house in which they were. Then there appeared to them tongues as of fire, which parted and came to rest on each one of them. And they were all filled with the holy Spirit and began to speak in different tongues, as the Spirit enabled them to proclaim" (Acts 2:2–4). This outpouring of the Holy Spirit produced immediate results. Previously in hiding, the apostles began preaching openly in the streets that Jesus Christ is Lord.

Peter ended the first Christian sermon that day by calling the crowd that had gathered to hear the apostles to "repent and be baptized...in the name of Jesus Christ for the forgiveness of your sins; and you will receive the gift of the holy Spirit" (Acts 2:38). As Jesus had promised, the Holy Spirit had arrived to remain with the apostles, empowering them to fulfill their mandate to "make disciples of all nations, baptizing them in the name of the Father, and of the Son, and of the holy Spirit" (Matthew 28:19).

The apostles themselves, anointed with the Holy Spirit at Pentecost, in turn imparted the Holy Spirit by laying their hands upon the newly baptized (Acts 8:15–17; 19:5–6). This apostolic imposition of hands is the origin of the sacrament of confirmation (DCN). Through it, baptized Christians are strengthened and obliged to continue the mission of Church, the mission of Christ himself, to evangelize the world (LG 11).

PROPHETS, KINGS, PRIESTS, AND THE HIGH PRIEST

The apostles were not the first ones to be anointed with the Holy Spirit. Jesus was anointed by the Holy Spirit from the moment of his conception in the womb of the Most Blessed Virgin Mary (Luke 1:35). That is why he is called "Christ." The title comes from the Greek word meaning anointed, and is a translation of the Hebrew title Messiah, or "anointed one." Jesus is Christ because he is anointed by the Holy Spirit as prophet, king, and priest. In Old Testament times, God provided for and communicated with his chosen people through these three significant offices or roles. In the New Covenant, Christ combines and perfectly fulfills all three offices in one person. This section briefly considers how Christ takes on the roles of prophet, king, and priest, and what these offices have to do with the sacrament of confirmation.

At the outset of his preaching ministry, Jesus read in the synagogue the words of the prophet Isaiah: "The spirit of the LORD God is upon me, because the LORD has anointed me; He has sent me to bring glad tidings...." (Isaiah 61:1). Having finished the reading, Jesus stated, "Today this Scripture passage is fulfilled in your hearing" (Luke 4:21). With these words, Christ claimed for himself the fullness of anointing with the Holy Spirit that was granted to the prophet Isaiah, along with the same prophetic mission: to preach good news.

The ancient Hebrew kings and priests received a literal anointing with oil, which was accompanied by an outpouring of the Holy Spirit. When Samuel used oil to anoint David as king of Israel, "the spirit of the LORD rushed upon David" (1 Samuel 16:13). Messiah, or "anointed one," became another name for the king of Israel in David's line (Psalm 132:10), and God promised David that his dynasty would last forever. That promise also is fulfilled in Christ, to whom God gave the throne of his ancestor David, so that his kingdom would have no end.

God also prescribed the anointing of ancient Israel's priests with oil, beginning with Moses' brother Aaron: "take the anointing oil and anoint him with it, pouring it on his head" (Exodus 29:7; see Leviticus 8:12). In the Old Testament, a succession of priests constantly interceded on behalf of the people in communicating with God. They offered sacrifices in the Temple of Jerusalem, including sacrifices of thanksgiving, atonement for sin, and praise. Christ offers the one sacrifice of himself on the cross, fulfilling all the sacrifices offered by priests of the old covenant year after year. Whereas the priests of the Old Testament died and were replaced by others, Jesus is anointed as "a priest forever" (Hebrews 5:6).

In this way, Christ combines and fulfills eternally in one person the three anointed offices of prophet, king, and priest. In the Old Covenant, these offices were held by different men. Kings, priests, and prophets all find their source and end in Christ the Messiah. Moreover, Christ's faithful are called Christians not only because they follow Christ, but also because they are anointed with oil and the Holy Spirit. With this anointing, the faithful carry on Christ's mission, empowered by the grace of sharing in his threefold role of prophet, king, and priest. As prophets, Christians proclaim and bear witness to the truth. As kings, Christians conquer the temptations of the world, the flesh, and the devil with the armor of virtues. As priests, Christians offer up an acceptable sacrifice of praise, in union with the perfect sacrifice offered by Christ the High Priest. All of this is possible with the gift of the Holy Spirit.

THE VISIBLE SIGN OF CONFIRMATION

God alone can bestow the divine gift of the Holy Spirit that enables the faithful to share in the threefold office of Christ as prophet, king, and priest. The Lord chooses to grant this gift through the ministers of the sacrament of confirmation on earth—first through the apostles, then through bishops, their successors. The apostles received the Holy Spirit at Pentecost, and imparted it by laying hands on the newly baptized. The bishops, as successors of the apostles, receive the sacramental power to pass on the Holy Spirit through confirmation. Therefore bishops are called the ordinary or original ministers of confirmation (LG 26; *CCC* 1312–1313; CT 7).

Whenever possible, the bishop should personally administer the sacrament. From ancient times, however, priests have been granted the faculty or permission to confirm the baptized faithful when necessary. Cases of necessity arise, for example, when a baptized Christian is about to die without having been confirmed. This leads to the question of the recipient of confirmation.

The recipient of the sacrament of confirmation is known as the candidate or the confirmand, from the Latin *confirmandus*, which simply means "one to be confirmed." Anyone who has been baptized but not yet confirmed can receive the sacrament. The Church considers confirmation so important that even an infant should receive the sacrament if in danger of death. Under less grave circumstances, a candidate for confirmation should have reached the age of reason (*CCL* 889 §2), and should meet four other criteria. A candidate must have:

+ The ability to profess the faith by renewing one's baptismal promises
+ The intention to receive the sacrament
+ Suitable instruction
+ A proper disposition

The matter or material element of confirmation is a perfumed oil called chrism, which the bishop consecrates during Holy Week each year. Chrism is so fundamental to confirmation that Eastern Churches designate the sacrament of confirmation with the word "chrismation." The main ingredients in chrism are olive oil and a fragrant plant extract called balm or balsam.

According to an allegorical interpretation proposed by Pope Eugenius IV (1431–1447), the oil signifies a good conscience, while the balm signifies a good reputation. Eugenius interpreted the "pleasing odor" (Leviticus 2:12) of the chrism used for confirmation in light of Saint Paul's exhortation to the Corinthians: "For we are the aroma of Christ for God among those who are being saved and among those who are perishing, to the latter an odor of death that leads to death, to the former an odor of life that leads to life" (2 Corinthians 2:15–16). Those with faith and charity find the reputation or "aroma" of Christians who live out the threefold office of Christ pleasing, but those who reject the Gospel find Christ's odor distasteful.

In the essential rite of confirmation, the minister anoints the confirmand by laying his right hand on the recipient's head. The hand-laying recalls the gesture with which the apostles conferred the Holy Spirit. The minister applies the chrism with his right thumb. The formulas used to confer confirmation or the sealing with the Holy Spirit have differed from time to time and place to place. These differences in form reflect complex historical developments. Even in the Latin Rite churches of the West, a common formula did not begin to emerge until the twelfth and thirteenth centuries.

The most common form in the Middle Ages is still used in the extraordinary form of the Roman Rite today: "I sign you with the sign of the cross and confirm you with the chrism of salvation. In the name of the Father and of the Son and of the Holy Spirit." In the ordinary form experienced by most Catholics, as the minister anoints the candidate on the forehead he pronounces the following formula: "be sealed with the Gift of the Holy Spirit." This formula is close to the Byzantine Rite, in which chrismation is conferred with the words, "the seal of the gift of the Holy Spirit."

CONTEXTS OF CONFIRMATION

Just as the form of confirmation has differed throughout Christian history, there also have been discrepancies with regard to the time when the baptized receive confirmation. Today, there are four different contexts in which a baptized Christian may receive the sacrament of confirmation.

The Rite of Christian Initiation of Adults (RCIA) provides instructions for two of these contexts: the reception into the Church's communion of an adult who has not yet been baptized, and the reception of an adult who has already been baptized. Adults who are baptized through the RCIA receive confirmation directly after baptism, and proceed to participate in the Eucharist. Baptized Christians from Protestant communities who are entering into full communion with the Catholic Church also receive confirmation through a process outlined in the RCIA.

The other two contexts for confirmation fall outside the scope of the RCIA, but are described in a distinct rite of confirmation: cases of danger of death, and the confirmation of youths baptized as infants or small children. When in danger of death, a baptized Catholic ought to be confirmed immediately. Most frequently, however, children or adolescents baptized as babies are confirmed through a process conducted by their parish or Catholic educational system. The rite of confirmation in their case takes place within the celebration of Mass wherever possible. Following the homily, the confirmation candidates renew their baptismal promises and the profession of faith.

A proper disposition is necessary if one is to fully participate in and therefore benefit from the sacrament. On the most basic level, the proper disposition entails being in the state of sanctifying grace that baptism brings about in the soul. If this state of grace has been lost through sin, it must be restored through the sacrament of penance—the topic of our fifth chapter.

Therefore the sacrament of penance should be employed as a means of preparing for the sacrament of confirmation. The candidate for confirmation ought to be prepared to assume the role of disciple and witness to Christ both inside and outside of the Christian community. As baptism is the sacrament of faith, confirmation is the sacrament of the confession of faith. In other words, the candidate should be prepared to undertake the mission of Christ and the Church, for his own salvation and that of the world: "For one believes with the heart and so is justified, and one confesses with the mouth and so is saved" (Romans 10:10). Suitable instruction through catechism classes is one way to prepare for this public confession. Growing closer to God through prayer and works of charity is another.

Sponsors make an important contribution to the formation of

the candidate for confirmation, both before and after actual reception of the sacrament. Sponsors share responsibility for preparing candidates with their families, the local clergy, and catechists. Sponsors also share the responsibility for continually guiding the confirmed Christian along the path of participation in the mission of Christ and the Church. In other words, sponsors guide candidates along the path of living as a true witness to Christ.

Each confirmand should have one sponsor, who must be a confirmed and practicing Catholic at least sixteen years of age. One of the baptismal godparents may, and if possible should, serve as the sponsor in order to highlight the connection between baptism and confirmation (*CCL* 874; 893). An enduring spiritual relationship arises between the sponsor and the newly confirmed Christian. When this spiritual relationship is cultivated well, the sponsor conscientiously seeks to help the newly confirmed live in fidelity to the Gospel, while the newly confirmed looks to the sponsor for guidance and accountability.

WHO CONFIRMS WHAT: THE GIFTS OF THE HOLY SPIRIT

This section addresses two distinct but closely related questions. The first is: Who is the agent of the sacrament of confirmation? In other words, who confirms what? The second issue has to do with gifts of the Holy Spirit that God imparts through this sacrament. These gifts perfect the Christian life, enabling it to become active and even heroic.

Although candidates may study catechesis and perform charitable service, confirmation must not be considered the result of human effort. Some, for example, view confirmation as a graduation ceremony from catechism classes, a reward for community service, or a demonstration that the candidate is able to contribute to the life of the Church. As with all sacraments, however, the initiative behind confirmation comes first and foremost from God.

Knowledge of the truths of the faith, works of charity, and participation in the Church's mission are all gifts of God's grace. In other words, the desire and the capacity to do good are gifts from God, and they precede and prepare the individual's good works. In the sacrament of confirmation, God pours out the gifts of the Holy Spirit that enable the Christian to participate more fully in Christ's threefold office as prophet, priest, and king. The prophet Isaiah first listed the seven gifts of the Holy Spirit:

+ Wisdom
+ Understanding
+ Counsel (or right judgment)
+ Fortitude (or courage)
+ Knowledge
+ Piety (or reverence)
+ Fear of the Lord

Isaiah was prophesying the coming of the Messiah, upon whom the Spirit of the Lord would rest (Isaiah 11:2–3). From the moment he was conceived by the power of the Holy Spirit in the womb of the Blessed Virgin Mary, Jesus possessed these gifts in their fullness (Luke 1:35). Therefore Jesus is known as the Anointed, the Messiah, the Christ from the moment of his conception. These three words indicate the same reality: Jesus, from the first moment of his existence, is anointed with the Holy Spirit and perfectly possesses the seven gifts of the Holy Spirit.

Through confirmation, the Christian participates more fully in Christ's anointing with the Holy Spirit and receives the same gifts of the Holy Spirit. The rite of confirmation emphasizes this reality of the Gift and the gifts of the Holy Spirit in a beautiful prayer that immediately precedes the essential rite of anointing.

All-powerful God, Father of our Lord Jesus Christ, by water and the Holy Spirit you freed your sons and daughters from sin and gave them new life. Send your Holy Spirit upon them to be their Helper and Guide. Give them the spirit of wisdom and understanding, the spirit of right judgment and courage, the spirit of knowledge and [piety] reverence. Fill them with the spirit of wonder and awe [fear of the Lord] in your presence. We ask this through Christ our Lord. (RC 42)

The Christian needs these gifts for the growth and perfection of the spiritual life begun in baptism. The seven gifts of the Holy Spirit enable the soul to live the moral life of the Beatitudes (Matthew 5:3–12). "The Beatitudes depict the countenance of Jesus Christ and portray his charity. They express the vocation of the faithful associated with the glory of his Passion and Resurrection; they shed light on the actions and attitudes characteristic of the Christian life" (*CCC* 1717). Pope Leo XIII expressed the powerful effects of the gifts of the Holy Spirit imparted at confirmation in terms of the Beatitudes: "By means of these gifts the soul is excited and encouraged to seek after and attain the evangelical beatitudes, which, like the flowers that come forth in the spring time, are the signs and harbingers of eternal beatitude" (DIM 11).

Our Lord takes the initiative when he grants divine gifts to the baptized in the sacrament of confirmation. God imparts the gift and the seven gifts of the Holy Spirit through the sacrament, enabling the Christian to learn, love, and live the Christian life according to the Beatitudes. Therefore confirmation should not be understood simply as a sacrament in which the Christian confirms his or her baptismal faith. Rather, God confirms and seals the Christian's faith in this sacrament with the gifts that make perfection of that faith possible. God confirms the Christian through the ministry of the bishop, the pastor of the local church. Participating in Christ's anointing with the Holy Spirit, the newly confirmed Christian also is fortified to participate in the mission of evangelization which Christ entrusted to the Church.

AN INVISIBLE GRACE—BOTH DEFENSIVE AND OFFENSIVE

The special grace of the Holy Spirit conferred at confirmation includes the strength to promote and defend the faith, enabling the newly confirmed to participate in the Church's mission of evangelization. "By the sacrament of confirmation," the Second Vatican Council teaches, the faithful "are endowed with a special strength of the Holy Spirit, and thus are more strictly obliged at once to spread and to defend the faith by word and by deed as true witnesses of Christ" (LG 11). Note the twofold emphasis on strength and obligation in these words.

On the one hand, confirmation enables an individual to spread the faith by word and deed. On the other hand, it enables the newly confirmed to defend and protect the faith by word and deed—even in the face of radical opposition. To use a military or sports analogy, the grace of confirmation is both offensive and defensive.

The grace for defense strengthens an individual to protect the faith from attacks that originate from temptations of the devil, the world, and the flesh. The great encyclical on the "Mystical Body of Christ" by Pope Pius XII declares: "By the chrism of Confirmation, the faithful are given added strength to protect and defend the Church, their Mother, and the faith she has given them" (MCC 18). In baptism, an individual receives spiritual power pertaining to personal salvation. In confirmation, the Christian receives power to engage in the spiritual battle against enemies of the faith.

The internal and external enemies of the faith are summarized with the trilogy of world, flesh, and devil. Through confirmation, baptized Christians gain strength needed to resist all of these enemies. In the words of Saint Alphonsus Liguori (d. 1787), the grace that confirmation imparts is "a special strength for fighting the battle of the Lord." The Christian needs this grace to defend personal faith and morality from the moment that he or she has the use of reason, since that is the moment when the attacks of the devil, the world, and the flesh intensify.

This lifelong battle is not only defensive; it also is offensive or missionary. The Second Vatican Council teaches that confirmation, along with the other sacraments of initiation, is the source of the apostolate of the laity (AA 3). The apostolate is marked by the lay Christian's role in bringing the Gospel into the world. Thus the council associates confirmation with apostleship and with a consecration that is both royal and priestly. This disposes the Christian to worship and bear witness to Christ.

In fact, confirmation perfects the common priesthood of the faithful received in baptism. Like baptism, confirmation imparts an indelible and unrepeatable spiritual mark on the soul that disposes the confirmed for fuller participation in divine worship. Therefore the Christian can be confirmed only once.

The sacrament of confirmation is a divine gift whereby God takes the initiative to confirm the baptized Christian's participation in the mission of Christ. This divine gift includes the Holy Spirit and the gifts of the Holy Spirit. This gift deepens the baptized Christian's participation in the divine life of the Trinity. This gift enables the Christian to grow in holiness, and to attain the heights of Christian perfection modeled in the Beatitudes.

The grace of confirmation is both defensive and offensive: it strengthens the Christian to defend and spread the faith by engaging in the Church's mission.

Finally, confirmation imparts an indelible character on the soul as a perpetual pledge of this divine gift to those who are disposed to fully participate in it.

PERSONAL PENTECOST

In the sacrament of confirmation, the Christian experiences a personal Pentecost. The apostles received the Holy Spirit at Pentecost, and passed it on to their successors through a laying-on of hands. The successors of the apostles, the bishops and priests associated with them, continue to confer the Holy Spirit through the sacrament of confirmation. Acting in the person of Christ, they administer the sacrament through the anointing with chrism, which constitutes the matter of confirmation.

The confirmand receives the gift of the Holy Spirit and the seven gifts of the Holy Spirit through this sacrament. Like the apostles, the newly confirmed are called to evangelize the world. The grace of the sacrament of confirmation strengthens the Christian to engage in this mission by defending the faith of the Church in Christ and by spreading that faith in the world. By the power of the Holy Spirit, the Christian proclaims in word and deed that "Jesus is Lord" (1 Corinthians 12:3), while pursuing the perfection of the Christian life outlined in the Beatitudes.

DISCUSSION QUESTIONS

1. *Why is Jesus called Christ?*

2. *What does this title have to do with the confirmation of Christians?*

3. *How is the divine institution of confirmation evident in sacred Scripture?*

4. *What is the matter and form of the sacrament of confirmation?*

5. *What does the Bible say about the odor of chrism and its meaning?*

6. *What are the gifts of the Holy Spirit?*

7. *How can the grace of confirmation be succinctly described?*

ABBREVIATIONS AND SOURCES

AA: Second Vatican Council, Decree on the Apostolate of the Laity *Apostolicam Actuositatem*. November 18, 1965.

AS: Congregation for Bishops. Directory for the Pastoral Ministry of Bishops *Apostolorum Succesores*. February 22, 2004.

CCC: *Catechism of the Catholic Church*. 1285–1321.

CCL: *Code of Canon Law*. Canons 879–896.

CT 7: Council of Trent, Session 7. Canons on Confirmation. March 3, 1547.

DCN: Pope Paul VI. Apostolic Constitution on the Sacrament of Confirmation *Divinae Consortium Naturae*. August 5, 1971.

DIM: Pope Leo XIII. "Encyclical on the Holy Spirit" *Divinum Illud Munus*. May 9, 1897.

LG: Second Vatican Council. Dogmatic Constitution on the Church *Lumen Gentium*. November 21, 1964.

MCC: Pope Pius XII, Encyclical on the Mystical Body of Christ *Mystici Corporis Christi*. June 29, 1943.

RC: Rite of Confirmation. In *The Rites of the Catholic Church*, vol. 1, pp. 469–515. Collegeville MN: Liturgical Press, 1990.

FOR FURTHER READING

A Catechism of Christian Doctrine: Prepared and Enjoined by Order of the Third Plenary Council of Baltimore, No. 2. (1885) Rockford, IL: TAN Books, 1977 reprint of 1933 edition by Benziger Brothers, Inc. The modern language rendition shown in the text for the "extraordinary form" of the Roman rite for confirmation is based on the version in this source, which uses archaic terms such as "thee" and "thou."

Corrada, Alvaro (Bishop of Tyler, Texas). *Pastoral Reflection on the Sacrament of Confirmation*. October 7, 2005.

Fisher, J.D.C. *Confirmation: Then and Now*. London, S.P.C.K., 1978.

Lampe, G.W.H. *The Seal of the Spirit: A Study of the Doctrine of Baptism and Confirmation in the New Testament and the Fathers*. London: Longmans, Green, 1951.

CHAPTER 4

The Most Holy Sacrament
The Perfection of Every Perfection

Christians have endowed the Eucharist with more titles than any other sacrament. The word "Eucharist" itself comes from the Greek word meaning "to give thanks," and reflects the fact that our Lord "gave thanks" at the Last Supper (Mark 14:23). The Second Vatican Council called this sacrament the "divine sacrifice of the Eucharist" (SC 2), the "sacrifice of the Mass" (SC 7, 12, 49), and "the mystery of faith" (SC 48). Pope Leo XIII emphasized that the "bread of life" (John 6:48) is God's gift, the chief of all gifts that God extends to humanity, and the gift "than which nothing can be more excellent or more conducive to salvation" (MC 5). Saint Thomas Aquinas aptly described the Eucharist as the "perfection of every perfection," and liturgical books refer to the "Most Holy Eucharist."

All of the sacraments are perfect and holy, but the Church calls the Eucharist the "Most Holy Sacrament" or the "Sacrament of sacraments" (*CCC* 1330) because of Christ's unique presence in it. Therefore this chapter will articulate carefully what the Church believes about Christ's presence in the Most Holy Sacrament. Just as many more titles of the Eucharist could be listed, so could much more be said about the sacred mysteries of the holy Mass. We cannot exhaust the mystery with our words, but we will endeavor to love it and understand it with the mind of the Church.

Beginning with the divine institution of the Eucharist, we will then explore the nature of Christ's presence in the sacrament. Consideration of Christ's presence leads to the sacrificial nature of the Mass and its relationship to the one sacrifice of Christ on the cross. In turn, Christ's sacrifice on the cross can be fully understood only in light of the other sacrifices recounted in sacred Scripture.

In the eucharistic sacrifice, the Christian participates in Christ's sacrifice on the cross. Therefore we must give careful attention to a proper understanding of sacramental participation in the Eucharist. In short, this chapter covers four main topics: the divine institution of the sacrament of the Eucharist, Christ's presence in this sacrament, the sacrificial character of the Eucharist viewed in light of the sacrifices of salvation history, and the effects of personal participation in the Eucharist.

THE INSTITUTION NARRATIVE AND THE ESSENTIAL RITE

At the heart of the Mass, in the midst of the eucharistic prayer, the celebrant recites the narrative of institution. This narrative recounts Christ's institution of the Eucharist at the Last Supper.

> On the day before he was to suffer he took bread in his holy and venerable hands, and with eyes raised to heaven to you, O God, his almighty Father, giving you thanks he said the blessing, broke the bread and gave it to his disciples, saying:
>
> *Take this, all of you, and eat of it, for this is my body, which will be given up for you.*
>
> In a similar way, when supper was ended, he took this precious chalice in his holy and venerable hands, and once more giving you thanks, he said the blessing and gave the chalice to his disciples, saying:

Take this, all of you, and drink from it: for this is the chalice of my blood, the blood of the new and eternal covenant, which will be poured out for you and for many for the forgiveness of sins. Do this in memory of me. (OM)

Catholics who regularly attend Mass easily recognize this narrative. Its words are drawn from the four biblical passages that relate Christ's institution of the Eucharist:

* Matthew 26:26–29
* Mark 14:22–25
* Luke 22:15–20
* 1 Corinthians 11:23–26

The words in capital letters are the words of institution or the words of consecration, or the words our Lord Jesus spoke at the Last Supper. They constitute the form of the essential rite, by which the bread and wine are consecrated and become the Body and Blood of Christ.

Our Lord spoke the words of consecration over the elements of bread and wine. For this reason, bread and wine are the matter of the sacrament of the Eucharist. Jesus drank grape wine, "the fruit of the vine" (Mark 14:25; Luke 22:18). According to the custom of his time, our Lord drank wine mixed with water. Since the Last Supper took place in the context of Jewish Passover celebrations, the bread in Jesus' hands was unleavened—in other words, it was made without yeast so that it did not rise. God commanded the Israelites to eat unleavened bread on the evening before their exodus from Egypt, and also to commemorate the event annually with a festival of unleavened bread (Exodus 12:15; Deuteronomy 16:3). Although the Roman Rite directs that unleavened bread be used for the Eucharist in Western liturgies, the Eastern Rite Churches tend to use leavened bread. Both of these traditions are ancient, and both validly celebrate the Eucharist.

The Lord spoke the words of consecration to "the apostles" (Luke 14:22) or "the Twelve" (Mark 14:17; Matthew 26:20). Christ had chosen this inner circle of followers at the start of his earthly ministry. With this same inner circle of twelve apostles, he reclined at the table for the Last Supper on the night before his passion and death. When the Lord commanded, "Do this in memory of me" (Luke 22:19; see also 1 Corinthians 11:24), he was not speaking to all his disciples, but only to the twelve apostles. Therefore the twelve apostles and their successors are the foundation of the priesthood that ministers the sacrament of the Eucharist. In other words, at the same moment our Lord instituted the sacrament of the Eucharist, he also instituted the sacrament of holy orders. The apostles' successors are the bishops, and they share the power to act as ministers of the Eucharist with the priests or presbyters of the Church.

In conclusion, the narrative of institution recited at Mass reveals the matter, form, and minister of the sacrament of the Eucharist. The matter is wheat bread and grape wine mixed with a small amount of water. The words of consecration constitute the form: "Take this all of you and eat of it…" and "Take this, all of you, and drink of it…" These are the very words that Christ spoke at the Last Supper. Following the words of consecration, the bread and wine are consecrated and changed into the Body and Blood of Christ.

NATURE OF THE REAL PRESENCE

The eucharistic presence of the Body and Blood of Christ is a central tenet of Catholic faith. When approaching a mystery so magnificent and so profound, one must be very careful with words. Over the centuries, the Church has developed a precise vocabulary for describing the nature of the Real Presence of Christ in the Eucharist.

We will focus on several particular phrases as foundational expressions of Christ's eucharistic presence. These phrases or formulas come from the Council of Trent, which infallibly articulated truths about the Eucharist in the sixteenth century. How are phrases delivered more than four hundred years ago still definitive for the faithful today? Pope Paul VI addressed this question in his Encyclical on the Eucharist *Mysterium Fidei*: "These formulas—like the others that the Church used to propose the dogmas of faith—express concepts that are not tied to a certain specific form of human culture, or to a certain level of scientific progress, or to one or another theological school" (MF 24). The formulas that express central mysteries of the faith are valid in all times and for all cultures.

Pope Paul VI insisted, moreover, that the truth of the mystery of the Eucharist cannot be accurately taught without mentioning the Council of Trent's teaching (MF 11). Although the council's expressions are perennially valid, they are not necessarily self-evident. The formulas with which the Church expresses her belief in the presence of Christ in the Eucharist must be carefully explained.

Under the guidance of the Holy Spirit, the Council of Trent succinctly expressed the Church's faith in the Real Presence as follows:

> ...in the august sacrament of the holy Eucharist, after the consecration of the bread and wine, our Lord Jesus Christ, true God and man, is truly, really, and substantially contained under the species of those sensible things. (CT 13)

Each part of this dense but profound statement of faith must be analyzed carefully. Note first the time frame. The reality of the bread and the wine on the altar before the consecration are not in question here. Rather, the statement acknowledges the presence of Christ after the words of consecration. After the consecration, the Church no longer talks about the nature or the reality of the bread and wine. As a matter of faith, the nature of bread and wine no longer exist after the consecration. The species, or appearances, of bread and wine, however, remain. *Species* is a Latin word meaning "appearances." The species or appearances are the sight, the smell, the feel, and the taste that present themselves to human senses. After the consecration, one still observes the species of bread and wine. Yet under those appearances that our senses perceive is the substance not of bread and wine but of the body and blood of our Lord Jesus Christ.

Now consider carefully the word "substantially," which appears in the formula cited above, and the related concepts of substance and substantial. In the context of the Church's teachings on the Real Presence of Christ in the Eucharist, these words carry a meaning that differs from our usual manner of speaking. Substantial presence regards not the appearances or sensible species of bread and wine, but the reality that underlies them. With the words of consecration, divine power changes the whole substance of the bread and wine into the whole substance of the Body and Blood of Christ.

To express the same thing differently, God changes the substance of bread and wine into the substance of the Body and Blood of Jesus Christ. No bread and no wine remain at all. By a sheer divine miracle, the appearances that usually indicate the substance of bread and wine remain after the consecration. The Church calls this change "transubstantiation" (CT 13; *CCC* 1376). Transubstantiation indicates that what appears to be bread and wine is not bread and wine at all after the consecration. Rather, the bread and wine have been changed into the Body and Blood of Christ. Because the species remain the same, transubstantiation is not accessible to the senses. The senses of sight, smell, touch, and taste cannot perceive the Real Presence. It can be perceived only through divine faith in the words of Christ: "This is my body...."

The other adjectives from the formula cited above, "truly" and "really," emphasize the reality of Christ's presence indicated by the word "substantially." To insist that Christ is really present in the Eucharist, or to speak of the Real Presence, is not to exclude the reality of other modes or ways in which the Lord is present. For example, one may speak of a general presence of Christ or of Christ's power in the Church's prayer and works of mercy, or in the Church's preaching. Within the Mass itself, Christ is present in the gathered congregation: "For where two or three are gathered together in my name, there am I in the midst of them" (Matthew 18:20). Christ is present also in the person of the ordained minister and in the proclamation of the Word. These modes of Christ's presence also are real. So the presence of Christ under the species of bread and wine "is called 'real' not to exclude the idea that the others are 'real' too, but rather to indicate presence par excellence, because it is substantial and through it Christ becomes present whole and entire, God and man" (MF 39; see also SC 7).

In a singular and most excellent sense, Christ is really present in the Eucharist because he is substantially present. The word "truly" excludes any symbolic interpretation of Christ's substantial and Real Presence under the species of bread and wine. Christ is truly present in the Eucharist in the same sense that we profess the Son to be "true God from true God" in the Creed. The Church employs terms such as true, truly, or veritable in such instances in order to insist that the concept under discussion is not intended to be understood symbolically. In doing so, the Church follows the example of Christ, who emphatically excludes symbolic interpretations of the Eucharist when he insists, "my flesh is true food, and my blood is true drink" (John 6:55).

The real, true, and substantial Presence in the Eucharist under the appearances of bread and wine pertains to all of Christ—Body and Blood, soul and divinity. The Council of Trent provides another fundamental formula to express this mystery: "immediately after the consecration, the veritable Body of our Lord, and His veritable Blood, together with His soul and divinity, are under the species of bread and wine" (CT 13).

When instituting the Eucharist at the Last Supper, the Lord specified that "this is my body" and "my blood." Christ did not mention his soul and divinity. How do we know that the soul and divinity of Christ also are present in the Eucharist? The soul of a living human being is always joined to his or her body and blood. When the soul separates from the body, the human being dies. The presence of Christ in the Eucharist is the presence of the living humanity of the resurrected Christ. Therefore his soul is joined to his Body and Blood, such that his humanity is complete.

This is the same humanity that was joined to the divinity of the Son of God in the Incarnation, that was born of the Blessed Virgin Mary, that suffered and died on the cross of Calvary, that rose from the dead in the resurrection, and that ascended into heaven to sit at the right hand of the Father. By virtue of the Incarnation, his humanity is forever united with his divinity. Therefore the substance of Christ's Body and Blood, joined to his soul because he is a living being, is always joined also to the divinity of the eternal Son of God. For this reason, under the smallest perceptible particle of either the consecrated species of bread or of wine, the whole Christ is present—Body and Blood, soul and divinity.

As a final note, the Real Presence of Christ continues or abides under the eucharistic species even after the Mass has concluded. Convinced of the reality of Christ's abiding presence, from earliest times the faithful have reserved the consecrated species and carried them to the sick and those in prison who were unable to attend Mass. Throughout the centuries, the Church also has honored the Real Presence with processions, adoration, and visits to the consecrated species.

Since the whole Christ is under the eucharistic species, the faithful owe the eucharistic presence the same worship and adoration that they owe to Christ himself, true God and true man—the worship of *latria* mentioned in the first chapter. For this reason, the Church continuously encourages worship and adoration of the sacrament c the Eucharist, even offering a rite for exposition and benedictio' the Most Holy Sacrament. Moreover, worship of Christ's Real Presence in the sacrament of the Eucharist both inside and outside of Mass should be intimately bound with participation in sacramental communion. In the words of Pope Benedict XVI: "Receiving the Eucharist means adoring him whom we receive" (SCar 66).

To summarize, after the consecration, Christ is really, truly, and substantially present under the appearances or species of bread and wine. This is to be understood literally, not symbolically. Through the divine miracle of transubstantiation, the substance or reality of the bread and wine are completely changed into the substance or reality of the Body and Blood of Christ. Through this change, the substance of bread and wine entirely cease to exist. Wherever one encounters the Body and Blood of Christ, one also encounters his soul and divinity, because of the reality of the Incarnation in the risen, living Lord. The Real Presence of Christ, whole and entire, remains in the sacrament even after the Mass has concluded. When Catholics worship the Eucharist, then, they worship not bread and wine but Christ, the Incarnate Son of God—Body and Blood, soul and divinity.

THE SACRIFICES OF THE OLD COVENANT

In the preceding section, we saw that Christ is present in the Eucharist. Through the Eucharist, the faithful participate in Christ's sacrifice so that they may rise with him to new life. In order to understand how the Mass is Christ's sacrifice, we will begin with the sacrifices of the Old Testament.

All of the sacrifices of the Old Testament point toward and find their fulfillment in Christ's perfect offering on the cross. Several of the ancient sacrifices, however, are of particular significance: the sacrifices offered by Abel, Abraham, and Melchizedek, and the sacrifices offered on Passover, at Mount Sinai, and on the Day of Atonement.

Among the ancient formulas found in Eucharistic Prayer I, also nown as the Roman Canon, is the following prayer by which the faithful beseech God the Father to accept the gifts they are offering at Mass:

> Be pleased to look upon them with serene and kindly countenance, and to accept them, as you were pleased to accept the gifts of your servant Abel the just, the sacrifice of Abraham, our father in faith, and the offering of your high priest Melchizedek, a holy sacrifice, a spotless victim. (OM)

This prayer connects the sacrifice of the Eucharist with three ancient sacrifices that the Lord regarded as acceptable: those offered by Abel, Abraham, and Melchizedek. Each of these sacrifices was a prophecy of the sacrifice of Christ, and each sheds light on the mystery of the eucharistic sacrifice.

Abel and his brother Cain offered the first sacrifices in salvation history (Genesis 4:2–5). Whereas the Lord rejected the sacrifice of Cain, he accepted the sacrifice of Abel. Abel offered a lamb from his flock, but he also offered something else: Abel offered himself to God in faith. The Epistle to the Hebrews explains that God accepted Abel's sacrifice because it was offered in faith by one who was righteous: "By faith Abel offered to God a sacrifice greater than Cain's. Through this he was attested to be righteous, God bearing witness to his gifts…." (Hebrews 11:4).

In jealousy and anger over God's acceptance of Abel's sacrifice, his brother Cain murdered him. Thus Abel's blood spilled out with the blood of the lamb that he offered. The blood of Abel's sacrifice, which the Lord heard crying out from the ground, was Abel's own blood (Genesis 4:10). The Epistle to the Hebrews relates Abel's offering to the sacrifice of Christ. The blood of Christ, according to Hebrews, "speaks more eloquently than that of Abel" (Hebrews 12:24).

The blood that Christ shed on the cross and offered at the Last Supper is the foundation of the new covenant. Throughout the history of the Chosen People, God sealed covenants with the blood sacrifices. One of the most significant is the one on Mount Sinai, where God sealed his covenant with Moses and the Israelites.

> Then, having sent certain young men of the Israelites to offer holocausts and sacrifice young bulls as peace offerings to the LORD, Moses took half of the blood and put it in large bowls; the other half he splashed on the altar. Taking the book of the covenant, he read it aloud to the people, who answered, "All that the LORD has said, we will heed and do." Then he took the blood and sprinkled it on the people, saying, "This is the blood of the covenant which the LORD has made with you in accordance with all these words of his." Moses then went up with Aaron, Nadab, Abihu, and seventy elders of Israel, and they beheld the God of Israel….Yet he did not smite these chosen Israelites. After gazing on God, they could still eat and drink. (Exodus 24:5–11)

The blood of this sacrifice sealed the covenant with which the Israelites committed themselves to the law revealed through Moses. By virtue of the old covenant, God established the Israelites as his Chosen People, committed to obeying his law as revealed through Moses. Christ understood the blood of his sacrifice on the cross as the foundation and seal of a new covenant, "the new covenant in my blood" (1 Corinthians 11:25; Luke 22:20). This new covenant establishes a new people of God.

The Epistle to the Hebrews insists that the blood of Christ is the blood of the new, second, and better covenant (Hebrews 8:6–8). The blood of the new covenant establishes the people of God, and the Church, which is committed to obeying the new law of the Gospel. Furthermore, both the sacrifice at Mount Sinai and the sacrifice of Christ bring about peace and communion between God and those offering the sacrifice. In order to enter into communion with God through the covenant at Mount Sinai, leaders of the Israelites partook or ate of the sacrifice. In a similar manner, Christ calls for the faithful to "eat " and "drink" of his sacrifice.

Long before the covenant at Mount Sinai, the Lord started to form his Chosen People by entering into a covenant with Abraham which was also sealed with a sacrifice. The Lord commanded Abraham to offer in sacrifice his beloved son, Isaac. According to Jewish and Christian traditions, Isaac willingly allowed himself to be offered in sacrifice. So this sacrifice is both the sacrifice of Abraham as a father and the sacrifice of Isaac, his son.

When they were about to offer this sacrifice, the Lord intervened. He prevented the killing of Isaac and provided a ram to offer in his place. Abraham's words to Isaac—"God himself will provide the sheep for the holocaust" (Genesis 22:8)—proved to be a prophecy of Christ, the "Lamb of God who takes away the sin of the world" (John 1:29, 36). Since a lamb is a young sheep and a ram is a male sheep, lamb, sheep, and ram can mean the same thing. God the Father provided his only begotten Son, Christ, as the lamb of the sacrifice. The ram Abraham found caught in the thicket took the place of his son, Isaac. Since all those who inherited God's covenant with Abraham would be Isaac's descendants, the chosen people were saved by the lamb killed in Isaac's place. In a similar manner, Christ, the Lamb of God, died to save the Chosen People of the new covenant—the Church—from sin and death.

Christ's identity as the Lamb of God also reflects the sacrifice of the Passover lamb. The blood of the Passover lamb around the doors of the Israelites' homes saved them from the tenth and worst plague, the death of the firstborn (Exodus 12:5–19). That plague led to the Israelites' final deliverance from slavery in Egypt. Once again, the Lord associated the salvation of his Chosen People from death with the blood of a sacrificed lamb. Christ is the "Lamb that seemed to have been slain" (Revelation 5:6), whose sacrifice delivers the faithful from the slavery of sin and death. That is why Christ's

Last Supper, passion, and crucifixion took place during the Passover observances in Jerusalem.

In addition to the Passover lambs, the Israelite priests of the Temple in Jerusalem also offered other sacrifices on a yearly, and even daily, basis. The sacrifices of the Day of Atonement or Yom Kippur merit particular mention, as they included the offering of goats, rams, and bulls as sacrifices for the forgiveness of sin. The High Priest then entered the sanctuary of the Holy of Holies, the most sacred part of the temple. There, he sprinkled the blood of the sacrifice on the altar and the Ark of the Covenant (Leviticus 16). According to the Epistle to the Hebrews, these sacrifices of the old covenant had to be repeated year after year because "it is impossible that the blood of bulls and goats take away sins" (Hebrews 10:4). By contrast, Christ shed his blood once and only once for the definitive forgiveness of sins:

> For Christ did not enter into a sanctuary made by hands, a copy of the true one, but heaven itself, that he might now appear before God on our behalf. Not that he might offer himself repeatedly, as the high priest enters each year into the sanctuary with blood that is not his own; if that were so, he would have had to suffer repeatedly from the foundation of the world. But now once for all he has appeared at the end of the ages to take away sin by his sacrifice. (Hebrews 9:24–26)

In fidelity to this clear testimony of sacred Scripture, the Catholic Church teaches that the sacrifice of the Mass cannot be understood as a repetition of the Christ's ultimate sacrifice.

One last sacrifice from the Old Testament remains to be considered: that of Melchizedek. This sacrifice does not involve any animals. Rather, Melchizedek's offering consists of bread and wine. Genesis describes Melchizedek as "a priest of God Most High," who blessed Abram with these words: "Blessed be Abram by God Most

High, the creator of heaven and earth; And blessed be God Most High" (Genesis 14:18–20). Note that several biblical passages associate Christ's priesthood with that of Melchizedek (Matthew 22:44; Mark 12:36; Luke 20:42–43; Hebrews 7).

Sacrifices were commonplace in the Old Testament, although some were far more significant than others. Christ's sacrificial self-offering on the cross is the fulfillment of all the sacrifices in the Old Testament—including the one-time sacrifices offered by Abel, Abraham, Melchizedek, and Moses, and the yearly sacrifices offered on the Passover and the Day of Atonement. The next link to establish is the connection between Christ's sacrifice on the cross and the divine sacrifice of the Eucharist.

THE SACRIFICE OF THE NEW COVENANT: ON THE CROSS AND ON THE ALTAR

In order to understand the Eucharist as a sacrifice, we considered several significant sacrifices of the Old Testament and linked them to the sacrifice of Christ. This section focuses on the sacrificial nature of the Eucharist, which derives from its connection with the sacrifice of Christ on the cross. To put it simply, Christ's sacrifice on the cross is one and the same with the sacrifice offered on the altar at Mass. The priest is the same, the victim is the same, and the purpose or effect is the same.

The priest who offers the sacrifice on the cross is the same priest who offers the sacrifice of the Mass—our Lord Jesus Christ. Christ acted as the priest who offered the sacrifice to God on Calvary. Jesus Christ also acts as the priest who offers the divine sacrifice of the Eucharist. Only by divine power can bread and wine be changed into the Body and Blood of Christ. The human priest at the altar brings about this change by virtue of the divine power of Christ working through him. Above all while offering the eucharistic sacrifice, the priest acts *in persona Christi*, or in the person of Christ. The phrase *in persona Christi* means far more than simply acting in the name of Christ or in his place, because nobody can take the place of Christ. Rather, *in persona Christi* "indicates a specific sacramental identification with 'the eternal High Priest' who is the author and principal subject of this sacrifice" (DC 8). Christ is the priest who offers the sacrifice of the Mass, just as he offered himself on the cross.

The victim offered in the crucifixion of our Lord also is the same victim offered in the divine sacrifice of the Mass—Christ, the divine Redeemer, "in his human nature with his true body and blood" (MD 70). Having discussed the Real Presence, we readily recognize that Christ is substantially present under the eucharistic species as he was substantially present on the cross.

Here an important distinction arises: the Mass is repeated, but the crucifixion is not. The sacrifice on Calvary took place once and only once. Christ "died to sin once and for all" (Romans 6:10). Now that Christ has risen from the dead, "death no longer has power over him" (Romans 6:9), so the shedding of his blood is impossible. In the Eucharist, on the other hand, the sacrifice of Christ on the cross is represented daily. Faithfully reflecting the Catholic tradition, Pope John Paul II insisted that the "Mass makes present the sacrifice of the Cross; it does not add to that sacrifice nor does it multiply it" (EE 12). This is a distinction in the manner or mode of the offering of the sacrifice on the cross and the sacrifice on the altar at Mass. The sacrifice itself, the Lord Jesus Christ in his human nature, remains one and the same.

Now let us consider the third point of unity between the sacrifice of Christ on Calvary and the divine sacrifice of the Mass: they share the same purposes or effects. Four such purposes stand out:

+ to glorify the Father
+ to give thanks to God
+ to forgive sins
+ to petition God for blessings

Praise. The first purpose or effect that Christ's sacrifice on the cross has in common with the sacrifice of the Mass is to accomplish the perfect praise of God. To give praise and glory to God is the first purpose of divine worship. Out of sheer love, the Christian joins in Christ's praise of the Father (Matthew 11:25) as this praise is consummated in the Lord's passion, death, resurrection, and ascension into heaven.

Thanksgiving. The second purpose of the sacrifice of Christ on Calvary and in the Eucharist is thanksgiving. Christ "gave thanks" at the Last Supper over the chalice (Mark 14:23), thereby setting the pattern for the Church's expression of thanks in the Eucharist. On the cross, the Body and Blood that Christ offered at the Last Supper became a thanksgiving to God offered by the faithful in union with Christ the High Priest. We are called to join in Christ's sacrifice by offering to the Father in thanksgiving all that we have and all that we are. This is expressed beautifully in the morning offering: "O Jesus, through the Immaculate Heart of Mary, I offer you my prayers, works, joys, and suffering of this day in union with the Holy Sacrifice of the Mass throughout the world." The Mass is the privileged moment for Christians to make this offering of thanks, in union with the acceptable offering of our Lord on Calvary.

Propitiation. The third purpose of both Christ's sacrifice on Calvary and the sacrifice of the Mass is to forgive sins and to reconcile human beings with God. To express this third purpose, the Church uses "propitiation" and a series of other terms, including "expiation" and "atonement," to express that we offer the Eucharist in hopes that God will be pleased with the sacrifice and accept it as atonement for our sins. In fact, the Father does accept the sacrifice of the Mass because it is the sacrifice of his beloved Son, Jesus Christ. God's acceptance of Christ's sacrifice brings about reconciliation between sinners and God, and therefore salvation from sin and death. Through the eucharistic sacrifice, the salutary effects of

Christ's crucifixion are applied for the remission of the lesser or venial sins that we commit daily, and the temporal penalty due to sin. Moreover, the sacrifice of the Mass is propitiatory for both the living and the dead. In other words, it benefits not only the living faithful who offer it or for whom it is offered on earth, but also the faithful who have died and are in purgatory, where they must render satisfaction for their sins.

Impetration. The fourth and final purpose of both Christ's sacrifice on Calvary and the sacrifice of the Mass is to petition God for "every grace and heavenly blessing" (OM). Just as we know that the Father accepts the sacrifice of his beloved Son Jesus Christ for the atonement of sins, we also know that the Father accepts the sacrifice of Christ for the petitions of the faithful. The term "impetration" expresses this purpose and effect of Christ's sacrifice. Impetration indicates a petition that is sure to be heard. With great confidence, the faithful know that God will hear any petition joined with the sacrifice of Christ.

Before concluding this treatment of the relationship between the sacrifice of Christ on Calvary and the sacrifice of the Mass, one final term should be addressed: memorial. Christ commanded the apostles, "Do this in memory of me" (Luke 22:19; see also 1 Corinthians 11:24). Thus the Lord instituted the sacrament of the Eucharist in part as a memorial of his sacrifice on the cross, whereby the memory of the crucifixion will be kept alive until the end of the world. Nonetheless the Mass is not merely a memorial of Christ's sacrifice, "but a true and wonderful though bloodless and mystical renewal of it" (MC 18). The Mass recalls Christ's sacrifice on the cross. But the Mass also renews or re-presents that sacrifice, applying its fruits to the individual Christian of every place and time. Through the Mass, the individual Christian benefits from and participates in the effects of Christ's one perfect sacrifice.

"By virtue of its close relationship to the sacrifice of Golgotha," wrote John Paul II, "the Eucharist is *a sacrifice in the strict sense*, and not only in a general way" (EE 13). As we have just seen, the relationship of the Eucharist to the sacrifice of Christ on the cross is precisely what makes the Eucharist a sacrifice. The sacrament of the Eucharist is a memorial of Christ's sacrifice on Calvary, and it also is much more. The divine sacrifice of the Eucharist shares the same priest, the same victim, and the same purpose as the sacrifice of Christ on Calvary: praise, thanksgiving, propitiation, and impetration. Only the manner of offering differs; the sacrifice on the cross was bloody, but because Christ cannot die again, the sacrifice of the Mass is bloodless.

PERSONAL AND ECCLESIAL EFFECTS OF THE EUCHARIST

We are still exploring the depths of the mysterious gifts that God in love and mercy gives in the Eucharist. In addition to the effects already considered, the Real Presence of Christ in the Eucharist brings about invisible graces that may be considered under two categories: personal and ecclesial.

Personal. On a personal level, the Eucharist brings about spiritual union of the individual Christian with Christ. "Whoever eats my flesh and drinks my blood remains in me and I in him" (John 6:56). The Eucharist, and especially the reception of holy Communion, effects the personal indwelling of which the Lord speaks. The word "communion" connotes this mutual indwelling between the believer and Christ. "The cup of blessing that we bless, is it not a participation in the blood of Christ? The bread that we break, is it not a participation in the body of Christ?" (1 Corinthians 10:16). Through eucharistic Communion, the believer participates in the Body and Blood, soul and divinity of Christ. Reflecting on this mystery, Pope Leo XIII asked, "what can be more honourable or a more worthy object of desire than to be made, as far as possible, sharers and partakers in the divine nature?" (MC 6).

Ecclesial. The ecclesial grace of the Eucharist brings about the union of believers with one another. Saint Paul expresses this effect of eucharistic Communion when he writes: "Because the loaf of bread is one, we, though many, are one body, for we all partake of the one loaf" (1 Corinthians 10:17). Eucharistic Communion, in short, is a fulfillment of Christ's prayer for his followers, "that they may all be one, as you, Father, are in me and I in you, that they also may be in us" (John 17:21). Through personal union with divine nature, Christians grow in ecclesial union with one another. Thus the Eucharist is at the foundation of the unity of the Church.

ACTUAL PARTICIPATION IN DIVINE LIFE

The Second Vatican Council emphatically expressed the Church's desire that the faithful should come to more devout and actual participation in the liturgy, and especially in the Mass (SC 14, 50). In the first chapter, we saw that each Christian's salvation depends upon his or her participation in the one sacrifice of Christ on the cross. The second chapter explored how recipients of baptism benefit from the saving power of Christ's crucifixion, death, and resurrection. This chapter has emphasized that participation in the sacrifice of the Mass is participation in the sacrifice of Calvary. The individual Christian's participation in the sacrifice of Christ, however, varies according to the personal disposition that he or she brings to the Eucharist.

What is the nature of this participation, and how can the believer attain it as fully as possible? This question can be answered in two stages. First is a consideration of participation in the Eucharist in general. Second is an inquiry into how to attain fruitful participation through forming the proper dispositions.

A worthy and fruitful reception of holy Communion unites one with God, such that the recipient participates in heavenly and divine life: "whoever eats this bread will live forever; and the bread that I will give is my flesh for the life of the world" (John 6:51). This is the deepest meaning of sacramental participation. The faithful, through God's merciful love and the merits of Christ's sacrifice on the cross, are given a share in the divine life. Baptism begins this life of sanctifying grace, confirmation strengthens it, and the sacrament of the Eucharist nourishes and sustains it. The Eucharist sustains the life of grace by helping the recipient overcome sin, and by strengthening and increasing faith, hope, and charity. In fact, the Eucharist strengthens every virtue: "in this most admirable Sacrament, which is the chief means whereby men are engrafted on the divine nature, men also find the most efficacious help towards progress in every kind of virtue" (MC 7). Participation in the Eucharist nourishes and sustains the Christian life of grace and virtue until it finds completion in the fullness of life with God in heaven.

What internal dispositions or thoughts and intentions foster such fruitful participation in the Eucharist? In his great encyclical on the sacred liturgy, *Mediator Dei*, Pius XII taught that the faithful should strive for the same dispositions as Christ when he offered himself on the cross.

> Now the exhortation of the Apostle Paul, "Let this mind be in you which was also in Christ Jesus" [Philippians 2:5], requires that all Christians should possess, as far as is humanly possible, the same dispositions as those which the divine Redeemer had when he offered himself in sacrifice: that is to say, they should in a humble attitude of mind, pay adoration, honor, praise and thanksgiving to the supreme majesty of God. Moreover, it means that they must assume to some extent the character of a victim, that they deny themselves as the Gospel commands, that freely and of their own accord they do penance and that each detests and satisfies for his sins. It means, in brief, that we must all undergo with Christ a mystical death on the cross so that we can apply to

ourselves the words of Saint Paul, "With Christ I am nailed to the cross" [Galatians 2:19]. (MD 81)

Since Christ was both the priest and the victim of his sacrifice on the cross, his dispositions at that moment were those of both the priest offering and the victim willingly being offered. Therefore the faithful should strive to offer themselves along with Christ as the victim of the sacrifice, and to join with Christ as priest in offering the sacrifice. Joining with Christ in "a mystical death" entails humbling oneself and offering oneself to God through a life of continuous prayer, devotion, and penance. As partakers in Christ's office as priest, the faithful offer themselves as victims or spiritual sacrifices united with the sacrifice of Christ. The more closely the individual Christian conforms his or her mind to the attitudes and dispositions of Christ, the more fruitfully that Christian participates in the eucharistic sacrifice.

This manner of participation in the eucharistic sacrifice can be achieved without necessarily receiving holy Communion. Even fuller, however, is participation in the Mass that includes reception of holy Communion. The Second Vatican Council recommended that fuller or "more perfect form of participation in the Mass whereby the faithful, after the priest's Communion, receive the Lord's body from the same sacrifice" (SC 55).

The priest must consume the Body and Blood of the Lord in order for the sacrifice of the Mass to be complete. The faithful in the congregation, on the other hand, need not receive holy Communion during any given celebration of the Mass. Yet the faithful derive most abundant fruit from the Mass when they participate both through taking on the dispositions of Christ, and through the reception of sacramental Communion. "The saving efficacy of the sacrifice," wrote Pope John Paul II, "is fully realized when the Lord's body and blood are received in communion" (EE 16).

Throughout history, the Church has desired and recommended that the faithful receive Communion when attending Mass. Since the Fourth Lateran Council in the year 1215, the Church has required the faithful to receive the sacrament of holy Communion at least once a year. This yearly Communion became known as one's "Easter duty," because it was received at Easter Mass after attending sacramental confession during Lent. As reverence for and understanding of the Real Presence of Christ in the Eucharist increased over the centuries, many of the faithful became reluctant or afraid to receive holy Communion. Yet the authentic teaching authority of the Church continued to encourage more frequent reception of holy Communion—for example, at the Council of Trent in 1551. Nonetheless, some clerics and one-sided theological movements set such high criteria for preparing to receive holy Communion that the faithful despaired of doing so.

In response, through the initiative of "the pope of the Eucharist," Saint Pius X (1903–1914), the Church more clearly articulated the requirements for receiving holy Communion. In order to receive holy Communion at the Mass, the faithful must meet only two criteria. First, they must not be conscious of being in a state of grave sin. This entails being free from mortal sin, and may require receiving absolution through the sacrament of penance before receiving holy Communion. The second condition is to have a right intention. A right intention entails three dispositions or desires: a desire to please God; a desire to be more closely united with God; and a desire to overcome personal sins, defects, and weaknesses (ST 2). As we prepare to receive our Lord in holy Communion, we should search our hearts to be sure that we are motivated by the love of God to grow closer to Christ, and to reject the sin that separates us from God.

THE PAST, PRESENT, AND FUTURE OF THE MOST HOLY SACRAMENT

"O Sacred banquet, in which Christ is received, the memory of His Passion is renewed; the soul is filled with grace, and a pledge of future glory given to us." The Church proclaims these words on the evening of the Solemnity of the Most Holy Body and Blood of Christ, also known as the feast of *Corpus Christi*. They highlight the significance of the Eucharist for the past, the present, and the future. The most holy sacrament transcends time. It draws together the past of salvation history, the present working of God's grace in the Church, and the future perfection of the faithful in Christ.

Past. With regard to the past, the Eucharist is a memorial of Christ's passion, death, and resurrection. The Eucharist is a real participation in the saving effects of Christ's sacrifice on Calvary. That sacrifice took place once. It was the fulfillment of the many sacrifices of salvation history that preceded it, including those of Abel, Abraham, Melchizedek, and Moses on Mount Sinai, and the sacrifices of Passover and the Day of Atonement.

Present. In the present, the divine sacrifice of the Eucharist re-presents the sacrifice of Calvary. The priest is the same, the victim is the same, and the purposes are the same. This sacrament offers the individual Christian the opportunity to participate in the sacrifice with which Christ established the new covenant in his blood. The faithful participate in this sacrifice by taking on the mind of Christ, priest and victim, as he offered himself on the cross.

In the present, the mind of the Christian who participates in the Eucharist with the proper disposition is filled with the personal and ecclesial graces of union with God and with other believers in the Church. The believer still more fully participates in the sacrament of the Eucharist by receiving holy Communion.

Future. The Real Presence of Christ—Body and Blood, soul and divinity—is under the species or appearances of bread and wine following the transubstantiation effected by the words of consecration. Sacramental participation in this Real Presence nourishes and sustains the Christian life of grace and virtue, which begins at baptism and confirmation, until it reaches future perfection in the kingdom of God. With a view to this future fulfillment of communion with God in heaven, the Eucharist is "a pledge of future glory."

In summary, this chapter highlighted the divine institution of the sacrament of the Eucharist, Christ's Real Presence in this sacrament, the sacrificial character of the Eucharist in light of the sacrifices of the old covenant and the sacrifice of Christ, the dispositions for fruitful participation in the Eucharist, the Eucharist's transcendence of past, present, and future. While the Church provides concepts and formulas that enable us to speak accurately about the Most Holy Sacrament of the Eucharist, no words can ever exhaust the reality of this great mystery.

DISCUSSION QUESTIONS

1. *What takes place within the Mass during the narrative of institution?*

2. *What dispositions enable one to fruitfully participate in the Eucharist?*

3. *Why is the presence of Christ in the Eucharist called the Real Presence?*

4. *What are the species of bread and wine?*

5. *What are the effects of the Eucharist?*

6. *What sacrifices from the Old Testament shed light on the divine sacrifice of the Eucharist?*

7. *What is the relationship between the sacrifice of Christ on Calvary and the sacrifice of the Mass?*

ABBREVIATIONS AND SOURCES

CCC: Catechism of the Catholic Church. 1322–1419.

CT 13: Council of Trent, Session 13. Decree Concerning the Most Holy Sacrament of the Eucharist. October 11, 1551.

CT 21: Council of Trent, Session 21. The Doctrine of Communion under both Kinds and the Communion of Little Children. July 16, 1562.

CT 22: Council of Trent, Session 22. Doctrine Concerning the Sacrifice of the Mass. September 17, 1562.

DC: Pope John Paul II. Letter on the Mystery and Worship of the Eucharist *Dominicae Cenae.* February 24, 1980. © 1980 Libreria Editrice Vaticana.

EE: Pope John Paul II. Encyclical on the Eucharist in Its Relationship to the Church *Ecclesia de Eucharistia.* April 17, 2003. © 2003 Libreria Editrice Vaticana.

MC: Pope Leo XIII. Encyclical on the Holy Eucharist *Mirae Caritatis.* May 18, 1902.

MD: Pope Pius XII. Encyclical on the Sacred Liturgy *Mediator Dei.* November 20, 1947.

MF: Pope Paul VI. Encyclical on the Eucharist *Mysterium Fidei.* September 3, 1965. © 1965 Libreria Editrice Vaticana.

OM: Order of the Mass. United States Conference of Catholic Bishops, 2010.

SC: Second Vatican Council. Constitution on the Liturgy *Sacrosanctum Concilium.* December 4, 1963.

SCar: Pope Benedict XVI. Post-Synodal Apostolic Exhortation on the Eucharist as the Source and Summit of the Church's Life and Mission *Sacramentum Caritatis.* February 22, 2007. © 2007 Libreria Editrice Vaticana.

ST: On Frequent and Daily Reception of Holy Communion *Sacra Tridentina.* December 20, 1905.

FOR FURTHER READING

Kereszty, Roch A., *Wedding Feast of the Lamb: Eucharistic Theology from a Historical, Biblical and Systematic Perspective.* Chicago: Hillenbrand Books, 2004.

Nichols, Aidan, *The Holy Eucharist: From the New Testament to Pope John Paul II.* Dublin: Veritas, 1991.

O'Connor, James T., *The Hidden Manna: A Theology of the Eucharist.* 2nd ed. San Francisco: Ignatius Press, 2005.

CHAPTER 5

The Sacrament of Penance
The Masterpiece of God's Goodness and Mercy

This chapter considers what Pope Pius XII called "the master-piece of God's goodness and mercy" (MN 52): the sacrament of penance, also known as the sacrament of reconciliation. The first section highlights Christ's divine prerogative to forgive sins and how he passed it on to the Church by instituting the sacrament and entrusting its power to priests and bishops. The concept of sin will be discussed next, before moving on to the essential rite of the sacrament and its effects. Finally, the time to approach penance and the main contexts in which it is received will be explored, before ending with a note about the sacrament's history.

INSTITUTION AND MINISTER:
"WHOSE SINS YOU FORGIVE ARE FORGIVEN"

Before physically healing the paralyzed man in Capernaum, Jesus healed his moral defects with the merciful and comforting words: "your sins are forgiven" (Mark 2:5). Upon hearing these words, the scribes uttered a shocked response: "He is blaspheming. Who but God alone can forgive sins?" (Mark 2:7). The scribes were correct in insisting that only God can forgive sins. By forgiving the paralyzed man's sins, Jesus did what only God can do. Then he proved his divine power in a striking and visible way through his miracles. By healing the paralytic, Jesus proved "that the Son of Man has authority to forgive sins on earth" (Mark 2:10).

All divine forgiveness of sin stems from Christ's passion, death, and resurrection. While this point has been made throughout earlier chapters, it cannot be overemphasized. Christ "suffered for sins" (1 Peter 3:18), and through his passion and death on the cross, merited the forgiveness of sins for all who are saved. Christ's sacrifice, as the previous chapter explains, was propitiatory: God accepts it for the remission or forgiveness of sin. As Saint Paul writes: "In him we have redemption by his blood, the forgiveness of transgressions" (Ephesians 1:7).

Christ provided that the divine forgiveness of sin he merited on the cross would still be available on earth after his ascension into heaven. When our resurrected Lord appeared to the apostles, he "breathed on them and said to them, 'Receive the holy Spirit. Whose sins you forgive are forgiven them, and whose sins you retain are retained'" (John 20:22–23). In consideration of Christ's words to Peter, the head of the college of apostles, the "power of the keys" includes the Church's power to forgive or retain sins: "I will give you the keys to the kingdom of heaven. Whatever you bind on earth shall be bound in heaven; and whatever you loose on earth shall be loosed in heaven" (Matthew 16:19).

With these words, Christ entrusted the power to forgive sins to the apostles, with Peter as their head. By doing so, Christ ensured that his power to forgive sins would remain active on earth through the ministry of the Church after his ascension into heaven. By the will of Christ and the power of the Holy Spirit, the apostles ordained bishops and priests as successors to their ministry of reconciliation. The sacred power conferred through ordination to the priesthood includes the prerogative to forgive sins; therefore only a priest or bishop can minister the sacrament of reconciliation. He does so *in persona Christi*, since God alone can forgive sins, and all forgiveness of sins stems from the passion and death of Christ.

This ministry is demanding for those who exercise it. They must unite themselves spiritually to the merciful intention of Christ. To effectively dispense God's forgiveness, priests undergo extensive preparation and training. They should be knowledgeable and discerning regarding human behavior. They must know and love the Church's teachings. They are called to pray for and do penance for the recipients of the sacrament (CCC 1466). Finally, priests and bishops must avail themselves of the same sacrament by approaching it frequently as recipients

The sacramental seal demands that every priest who hears confessions must keep absolute secrecy about sins confessed. In the words of the *Code of Canon Law*, "The sacramental seal is inviolable; therefore it is absolutely forbidden for a confessor to betray in any way a penitent in words or in any manner and for any reason" (*CCL* 983, 1). The Church so strictly regards and protects the sacramental seal that a priest who violates it is subject to the severest penalty the Church possesses—excommunication. In light of how strictly the Church defends the privacy of the confessional, the faithful may approach the sacrament of penance with complete confidence in the minister's discretion.

Let us take a moment to review. Our Lord Jesus Christ demonstrated during his earthly ministry his divine power to forgive sins. After the resurrection, Christ instituted the sacrament of reconciliation by entrusting Peter and the apostles with the power of the Holy Spirit to forgive sins. The bishops and priests who succeed the apostles possess the power to act as ministers of the sacrament of reconciliation by virtue of their ordination. The charge to reconcile sinners by ministering Christ's mercy in this sacrament is among the most difficult of the roles that the priest must fulfill.

POST-BAPTISMAL SIN AND THE ONGOING CALL TO CONVERSION

The recipient of the sacrament of penance (the penitent) already has been baptized. In the sacrament of penance, the penitent confesses post-baptismal sins. Therefore this sacrament can best be understood in light of post-baptismal sin and the Christian's ongoing call to conversion. We will see that post-baptismal sin necessitates continuous conversion—that is, ongoing repentance and turning to the Lord.

As we learned in the second chapter, the sacrament of baptism effects the forgiveness of sin. This includes both original and personal sin, as well as the temporal and eternal penalty owed for sin. After receiving the sacrament of baptism, the new Christian need not immediately perform any acts of penance because the temporal penalty of sins committed before baptism is erased forever. Concupiscence—the frailty and inclination to sin with which we struggle throughout our lives—remains after baptism. Through wrestling with concupiscence, and by the grace of Christ, conquering it, the Christian is rewarded with an eternal crown.

Unfortunately the Christian does not always conquer concupiscence. Experience teaches that Christians fall and sin after baptism. Because we fall daily, we pray daily for forgiveness: "forgive us our trespasses, as we forgive those who trespass against us." The trespasses mentioned in the Lord's Prayer indicate lesser or venial sins that weaken and wound charity in the Christian soul. When we repent of these venial sins, God forgives them through means such as prayer, self-denial, acts of charity, and participation in the Mass.

Many Christians commit not only lesser or venial sins, but also serious or mortal sins. This includes Saint Peter himself, who committed the serious sin of apostasy when he denied our Lord three times. Serious or mortal sins destroy charity and the life of grace begun at baptism in the Christian soul. Moreover, mortal sins committed after baptism are not forgiven simply through prayer, self-denial, charity, and participation in the divine sacrifice of the Mass. Without God's forgiveness, the spiritual death of mortal sin will lead to external exclusion from the presence of God in heaven. The Lord in his goodness and mercy offers that forgiveness in the sacrament of penance. Only through the sacrament of penance can penitents find forgiveness and escape spiritual death and exclusion from heaven.

The integrity of the baptized Christian who is in a state of grace has been compared to that of a ship that is sound and seaworthy. The grace of God flowing from baptism carries the Christian soul through the tumultuous earthly life with its trials and temptations. Serious sin committed after baptism is like a shipwreck, wherein the Christian risks drowning and never reaching the safe port of heaven. In his mercy, God provides penance as a "second plank after shipwreck," to use the words of Saint Jerome (d. circa 420) and Saint Thomas Aquinas (d. 1275). Like a plank of wood that enables the shipwrecked sailor to remain afloat, penance provides another chance for the Christian to be saved by the grace of Christ and to arrive at the final destination of eternal life in heaven.

Seizing upon the "second plank" of the sacrament of penance requires recognition of the reality of personal sin and the need for repentance. Saint Peter again serves as an illustration: immediately struck by his sin of denying the Lord, Peter bitterly repented. Not all Christians are as sensitive to the reality of sin as Peter. Therefore the call to repentance that accompanies the call to baptism (Acts 2:38) continues for those who have been baptized. As Christ dictates to the church in Laodicea, so he continuously addresses all the faithful: "Be earnest...and repent" (Revelation 3:19).

To conclude, there are two categories of post-baptismal sin: venial and mortal. Venial sin wounds charity. Serious sin, like a shipwreck, destroys charity and the life of grace in the Christian soul. That life can only be restored by the "second plank," the sacrament of penance. An individual can only have recourse to the sacrament of penance, however, if he or she recognizes the reality of personal sin. For this reason, the Church issues a call to constant repentance and conversion to Christians.

CRISIS IN THE SENSE OF SIN

Repentance is not possible if the Christian is unaware of his or her personal sin. Fewer and fewer Christians are able to admit that they are sinners who continuously stand in need of God's mercy. Popes from the mid-twentieth century drew attention to a decline in the sensitivity to sin that enables recognition of one's need for God's forgiveness. Pope John Paul II in particular frequently warned against the "loss of the sense of sin" (for example, RecP 18). The crisis in the sense of sin has in turn led to a crisis in the sacrament of penance.

The loss of the sense of sin is not unique to the modern-day world. John the Apostle warned the first generations of Christians against it: "If we say, 'We are without sin,' we deceive ourselves, and the truth is not in us. If we acknowledge our sins, he is faithful and just and will forgive our sins and cleanse us from every wrongdoing." (1 John 1:8–9) With these words, the First Epistle of John emphasizes a truth of the faith: We are all sinners, and we all stand in need of the forgiveness of God. Several factors contribute to the loss of the sense of sin illustrated by the attitude and the words, "we are without sin."

The first of these is a loss of the sense of God, or belief in God. As John the Apostle indicates, belief in God's forgiveness and in one's personal need for that forgiveness, go hand-in-hand. Why? Because sin is first and foremost an offense against God: "Against you alone have I sinned; I have done such evil in your sight" (Psalm 51:6).

When belief in God decreases as cultures become predominantly secular, so, too, does the authentic sense of sin. In addition to the secularization of nations, families, and individuals, moral relativism (the default morality taught in most institutions of higher education) obscures the sense of sin by insisting that there is no universal standard of moral behavior that applies to all human beings.

During the past half-century, misguided theologians have exacerbated the challenge of moral relativism by developing misleading theories that undermine the reality of serious sin. As the consistent and timeless moral teachings of the Church, especially in the area of sexual ethics, grow increasingly unpopular and even openly mocked, Christians themselves are tempted to reject the moral law.

The sense of sin is rooted in the conscience. The factors that contribute to the loss of the sense of sin deaden the conscience. According to the Second Vatican Council, the moral conscience is "the most secret core and sanctuary of a man," where "he is alone with God, Whose voice echoes in his depths." The council continues: "In a wonderful manner conscience reveals that law which is fulfilled by love of God and neighbor" (GS 16). As the Christian's conscience is eclipsed, his or her individual relationship with God and neighbor is compromised, torn asunder, and even destroyed. Charity—the love of God and of neighbor—cannot flourish when wounded or killed through sin. As a result, the unrepentant Christian with a deadened conscience cannot fruitfully participate in divine worship.

The sacrament of penance is the key to renewing a Christian life led by a sound and upright conscience. Yet the current crisis with regard to sin has led to a crisis in the sacrament of penance. The sacrament of penance must be promoted in the Church. Penance is needed to enliven the Christian conscience so that it can once again become the sanctuary of an intimate and loving encounter between God and the individual Christian.

ESSENTIAL RITE

Valid reception of the sacrament of reconciliation demands three acts on the part of the recipient or penitent, and one act on the part of the minister. The three acts of the penitent are:

+ Contrition
+ Confession
+ Satisfaction

Between the confession and the satisfaction of the penitent, the ministering bishop or priest utters the words of the sacramental form, that is, the absolution. This section addresses each of the four elements of the essential rite of the sacrament of penance: contrition, confession, absolution, and satisfaction.

Contrition. Contrition is the most important act performed by the penitent. Contrition first entails repentance, which is grief and detestation for the sins one has committed. Contrition also includes the intention not to sin in the future, that is, a sincere desire to change. In the New Testament, the Greek word *metanoia* expresses this notion of repentance and conversion. Such a change of heart is at the very core of the Gospel message preached by Christ: "Repent, for the kingdom of heaven is at hand!" (Matthew 3:2; see also Mark 1:15). The *metanoia* preached by Christ entails a profound conversion of one's whole being, whereby the person begins to consider, judge, and arrange his or her entire life around the love of God and the fulfillment of God's law. Although it wells up from within the individual, *metanoia* is a gift from God.

Contrition can be perfect or imperfect. Perfect contrition is complete sorrow for sin, motivated solely by love for God. Imperfect contrition or attrition springs from less perfect motives, such as the fear of punishment. Nonetheless, imperfect contrition is real contrition, and it suffices for a valid sacramental reconciliation. United with confidence in divine mercy along with a desire to receive the sacrament of reconciliation, contrition prepares one who has fallen after baptism for the remission of sins.

Confession. The penitent's second act, the confession of sins, must be spoken. The Prodigal Son illustrates verbal confession welling up from internal sorrow for sins and conversion of heart when he cries out, "Father, I have sinned against heaven and against you; I no longer deserve to be called your son" (Luke 15:21). The Apostle James exhorts the faithful to "confess your sins to one another and pray for one another, that you may be healed" (James 5:16; see also 1 John 1:8–9).

What sins should be confessed? The penitent must verbally confess all mortal sins to the priest, if possible by name and number. The Church strongly recommends that penitents also confess venial sins. The practice of regularly confessing even venial sins often proves beneficial to the individual Christian's spiritual growth.

Absolution. Having heard the confession of the penitent and judging it to be a genuine reflection of repentance and a desire for conversion, the minister utters the sacramental form whereby he grants absolution from sin. The key words of the sacramental form begin, "I absolve you…." *(ego te absolvo).* These words are found within a larger formula that differs between the ordinary and the extraordinary use of the Roman Rite. The extraordinary form follows:

> May our Lord Jesus Christ absolve you: and I by his authority absolve you from every bond of excommunication, suspension [for clerics only] and interdict, insofar as I am able, and you need it. And finally, I absolve you from your sins, in the name of the Father, and of the Son, and of the Holy Spirit. Amen. (See RR 309–311)

In extreme cases, such as when death appears imminent, a shorter form may be used: "I absolve you from all censures and from your sins, in the name of the Father, and of the Son, and of the Holy Spirit. Amen" (see RR 311). The ordinary form of the sacrament of penance adds an emphasis on the ministry of the Church:

> God, the Father of mercies, through the death and resurrection of his Son, has reconciled the world to himself and sent the Holy Spirit among us for the forgiveness of sins. Through the ministry of the Church may God give you pardon and peace. And I absolve you from your sins in the name of the Father, and of the Son, and of the Holy Spirit. (RP 46)

Here again, a shorter form may be used when necessary: "I absolve you from your sins in the name of the Father, and of the Son, and of the Holy Spirit" (RP 65).

Before uttering the words of absolution, the priest provides the penitent with a penance. Active penance or satisfaction—the "fruit" worthy of *metanoia* (Matthew 3:8; Luke 3:8–9; John 15:2)—is the final act required on the part of the penitent for a complete and valid sacramental confession. Works of satisfaction fall into three categories. First is the penance imposed by the judgment of the minister of the sacrament. The priest must, within the bonds of reason and prudence, impose salutary and suitable satisfactions. Second, the penitent may willingly and purposefully undertake works of fasting or self-denial, almsgiving, and prayer in order to atone for personal sins. Biblical phrases such as "beating their breasts" (Luke 23:48; 18:13) and "sackcloth and ashes" (for example, Luke 10:13; Jonah 3:6) illustrate the demanding nature of personally undertaken penance driven by *metanoia*. Devout participation in the liturgy of the Church, and especially the divine sacrifice of the Eucharist, also can fall into this second category of satisfactions. Finally, the trials and sufferings of life, if borne patiently by the penitent, may be offered as satisfactions for sin.

Works of satisfaction or penance serve several purposes. They help the individual penitent progress in the spiritual life by discouraging sin, encouraging caution and vigilance in this regard, and purging the remnants of sinful attachments. Satisfaction fosters and actualizes life-changing conversion. With regard to justice, works of satisfaction make amends for the temporal punishment incurred by all sin committed after baptism. Moreover, this is a necessary preparation for entering into the kingdom of God. The penitent Christian who dies in the grace and forgiveness of God without having rectified the wrongs of personal sin here on earth, must render such satisfaction in purgatory before entrance into heaven.

EFFECTS OF THE SACRAMENT

The effects of the sacrament of penance are threefold: forgiveness of sins, reconciliation with God and the Church, and spiritual resurrection of the life of grace in the Christian soul.

Reconciliation. The sacrament of penance brings about reconciliation between God and the sinful Christian. Although the individual's sin affects others, all sin is first and foremost an offense against God. As a result, it compromises the relationship between God and the individual. The sinner cannot bear to be in God's presence: "Depart from me, Lord, for I am a sinful man" (Luke 5:8). The rupture sin causes in the relationship between God and his creatures dates back to the Fall of Adam and Eve (Genesis 3:8). Through the sacrament of reconciliation, the merciful God restores the personal relationship with him that is lost through sin. Reconciliation with God, moreover, entails reconciliation with the body of Christ, the Church.

Forgiveness. The second effect of the sacrament of penance is the forgiveness of sin, a necessary prerequisite for reconciliation with God. In the sacrament of reconciliation, Christ forgives both mortal and venial sins. The sacrament of reconciliation also remits the eternal punishment owed for mortal sin. Eternal punishments—hell and its torments—are distinct from temporal punishments. Temporal punishments are rendered by penance on earth or in purgatory. Through the forgiveness of sins, God restores sanctifying grace to those who lost it through mortal sin, thereby opening the way to heaven for faithful penitents.

Spiritual Resurrection. The result of God's forgiveness and reconciliation in the sacrament of penance is a spiritual resurrection. The sinner lost the divine life of grace that began at baptism. Through this sacrament, the repentant Christian once again lives in God's grace, as Christ restores him or her to the dignity and blessings granted to the children of God. Such blessings include preparation for the final judgment and the hope of entrance into the eternal beatitude of heaven.

The sacrament of reconciliation also increases the penitent's spiritual strength to continue to battle evil, fight temptation, and actively engage in the Church's mission to evangelize the world.

Finally, the penitent often experiences peace and serenity of conscience. Such divine consolation results from the confidence that the penitent's sins have been forgiven and that the relationship with God has been restored.

Such are the effects of the sacrament of penance. Through this sacrament, God forgives the penitent's sins and the eternal penalty owed for sin. The forgiveness of sin makes possible the second effect of penance: the reconciliation of the individual penitent with God and the Church. Finally, the forgiven sinner experiences a spiritual resurrection. This resurrection allows the sinner to once again participate in Christ's mission entrusted to him at the time of baptism and confirmation.

TIME TO REPENT: WHEN TO APPROACH THE SACRAMENT OF PENANCE

The Church requires that baptized Christians having attained the age of discretion attend sacramental confession at least once a year. This is a minimum requirement to ensure that Catholics have regular recourse to the masterpiece of God's goodness. Lent is an especially appropriate time for contrition and penance. One who has committed mortal sin, on the other hand, must approach the sacrament of penance as soon as possible. Since being in a state of mortal sin renders fruitful participation in the Eucharist impossible, a Christian in such a state may not approach holy Communion until receiving absolution in the sacrament of penance

Because of its effect in purging the faithful of sin, the sacrament of penance is recommended for the faithful who have reached the age of reason before they receive any other sacrament except baptism. Children must attend sacramental reconciliation before receiving their first holy Communion. It is an indispensable part of preparation for the sacraments of confirmation, holy orders, and matrimony. Sacramental reconciliation also is offered wherever possible in conjunction with the anointing of the sick.

In dangerous, difficult, or challenging circumstances, the sacrament of reconciliation helps an individual stay on the path of spiritual progress toward God. It enables the faithful to remain focused on the love of God and the promises of eternal life in heaven, while offering the trials of the world as satisfaction in reparation for sins. In the midst of comfort, joy, and triumph, this sacrament offers the grace to avoid the indifference and laxity that can lead to serious sin, even in someone as richly blessed as King David.

CONTEXTS OF CONFESSION

The Church's rite of penance for a single penitent is simple. It focuses on the penitent's confession of sins and the absolution granted by the minister. The ordinary form may include a reading from Scripture, although this occurs infrequently. In addition to an integral confession between one priest and one penitent, the ordinary form provides for two further contexts in which absolution might be rendered.

The first is called the "Rite for Reconciliation of Several Penitents with Individual Confession and Absolution." This is a public penitential service, complete with scriptural readings and a homily. Time is provided for private confessions, typically with a number of confessors available, after which the faithful come together for a final prayer, blessing, and dismissal. A number of parishes offer such services during Lent or parish missions.

The "Rite for Reconciliation of Several Penitents with General Confession and Absolution" provides another context for absolution. In this rite, the minister grants any number of penitents absolution after a general confession of sins. The individual confession of sins on the part of each penitent does not take place because time is too short and a sufficient number of ministers is lacking. The Church provides this rite of general confession and general absolution as an extraordinary means to be used only in exceptional circumstances or cases of grave necessity. The first such circumstance occurs when death is imminent and the priests do not have sufficient time for individual confession, as for example on the top floor of a burning building. The second such circumstance occurs "when, in view of the number of penitents, sufficient confessors are not available to hear individual confessions properly within a suitable period of time, so that the penitents would, through no fault of their own, have to go without sacramental grace or holy communion for a long time" (RP 31; see the clarification in MisD 31). The employment of this rite for general absolution when it is not necessary unfortunately contributes to the abandonment of individual confessions. Yet even those who receive general absolution are obliged as soon as possible, should they survive, to attend the sacrament of penance (RP 34). "Individual and integral confession of grave sins followed by absolution remains the only ordinary means of reconciliation with God and with the Church" (*CCC* 1484, 1497).

PARTING WORDS

A not-at-all pious individual once told me that he would enjoy being Catholic because he could do whatever he wanted and then attend confession to make it right. This is a mistaken notion on many levels.

First, contrition—including the resolve to sin no more—is a necessary part of the sacrament. The sacrament simply is not valid where contrition is lacking. Second, this sacrament is an integral part of the ongoing conversion, the habitual *metanoia* that marks growth in the Christian spiritual life. The sacrament of penance increases the Christian's desire to please God, and encourages the faithful to grow closer to Christ by shedding sinful habits and living in accordance with the law of the Gospel. Third, God's forgiveness is not a license to sin. "Shall we persist in sin that grace may abound? Of course not! How can we who died to sin yet live in it?" (Romans 6:1–2).

As a final note, do not assume that the sacrament of penance will be available just before death, so that the remainder of life can be passed in serious sin without fearing the loss of heaven. God has revealed "neither the day nor the hour" (Matthew 25:13) of judgment, so vigilance against sin is ever necessary. Repent now, "for the kingdom of heaven is at hand" (Matthew 3:2). Thus our Lord's tender words of forgiveness are accompanied with a warning against further sin: "Go, and from now on do not sin any more" (John 8:11).

DISCUSSION QUESTIONS

1. *What are the scriptural foundations of the sacrament of penance?*

2. *What are the three requirements on the part of the penitent for a valid sacramental confession?*

ABBREVIATIONS AND SOURCES

CCC: Catechism of the Catholic Church. 1420–1498.

CCL: Code of Canon Law. Canons 959–997.

GS: The Second Vatican Council. Pastoral Constitution on the Church in the Modern World *Gaudium et Spes.* December 7, 1965.

MisD: Pope John Paul II. Apostolic Letter issued *motu proprio* On Certain Aspects of the Celebration of the Sacrament of Penance *Misericordia Dei.* April 7, 2002.

MN: Pope Pius XII. Apostolic Exhortation to the Clergy *Menti Nostrae.* September 23, 1950.

RecP: Pope John Paul II. Post-Synodal Apostolic Exhortation On Reconciliation and Penance in the Mission of the Church Today *Reconciliatio et Paenitentia.* December 2, 1984.

RP: Rite of Penance. In *The Rites of the Catholic Church*, vol. 1, pp. 519–629. Trans. International Committee on English in the Liturgy. Collegeville MN: Liturgical Press, 1990.

RR: *The Roman Ritual: In Latin and English With Rubrics and Planechant Notation,* vol. 1, *The Sacraments and Processions.* Trans. and ed. Philip T. Weller. Milwaukee: Bruce, 1950. The modern language rendition shown in the text for the "extraordinary form" of the Roman rite for absolution at confession is based on the version in this source, which uses archaic terms such as "thee" and "thou."

FOR FURTHER READING

Hahn, Scott. *Lord have mercy: The Healing Power of Confession.* New York: Doubleday Religion, 2003.

Lowery, Mark. *Living the Good Life: What Every Catholic Needs to Know About Moral Issues.* Ann Arbor, MI: Servant Publications, 2003.

Pope John XXIII. Encyclical on the Need for the Practice of Exterior and Interior Penance *Paenitentiam Agere.* July 1, 1962.

CHAPTER 6

Anointing of the Sick
Suffering and Dying with Christ

The sacrament of anointing of the sick, also known as extreme unction, originated in Christ's divine power to forgive sins and to heal sickness. This chapter will begin by considering Christ's ministry as the divine physician who heals both body and soul. Then we will explore the institution of the sacrament of anointing of the sick, by which our Lord entrusted his power to forgive and to heal to the Church. The elements of the essential rite of the sacrament of anointing will be set forth next, followed by a treatment of its invisible grace or effects. The final section of the chapter is devoted to the recipient of anointing of the sick and the contexts in which the sacrament is administered.

CHRIST THE PHYSICIAN:
INSTITUTION OF THE SACRAMENT OF ANOINTING OF THE SICK

Christ's power as divine physician provides a key to understanding the sacrament of anointing of the sick. This section reflects on that power and how the Lord entrusted it to the ministers of the Church by instituting this sacrament.

Christ the physician associates the forgiveness of sins and healing of the soul with the healing of the body. This connection reflects the fact that illness, suffering, and death are consequences of sin. "'That you may know that the Son of Man has authority on earth to forgive sins'—he said to the man who was paralyzed, 'I say to you, rise, pick up your stretcher, and go home'" (Luke 5:24). We already have seen the origins of the sacrament of penance in this passage. The verse also reveals the origins of the sacrament of anointing the sick. The onlookers recognized that Jesus was claiming divine power by presuming to forgive the paralytic's sin. They also recognized that Jesus was demonstrating divine power by healing the paralytic. Just as God alone forgives sins, no physical ailment is healed without God's power at work. Therefore the "works" of healing that Jesus performed demonstrate his divine identity: "The works that the Father gave me to accomplish, these works that I perform testify on my behalf that the Father has sent me" (John 5:36).

Jesus' works of healing were so prominent in his earthly ministry that believers called Christ "the divine physician" from the earliest days of the faith. This title recalls the Lord's response to the pharisees who grumbled against him for associating with sinners: "Those who are well do not need a physician, but the sick do" (Matthew 9:12; Mark 2:17). With these words, our Lord claims the role of physician, and demonstrates that his mission includes the healing of sin and illness. Many of the crowds that followed Jesus during his earthly ministry were attracted to him only because of the power he demonstrated through innumerable works of healing. As his reputation for healing spread, people brought their sick to Christ just about everywhere he went (see Matthew 4:24, 14:35; Mark 6:55–56). "He laid his hands on each of them and cured them" (Luke 4:40).

Christ imparts a share in his role as divine physician to his disciples. "Cure the sick," he commands the twelve apostles (Matthew 10:8), much as he shares with them the ability to forgive sins (see John

20:23). After his resurrection, the Lord indicates that "in my name" believers "will lay hands on the sick, and they will recover" (Mark 16:17–18). There is no reason to think that our Lord was speaking only figuratively here, or that he had in mind only the healing of the spirit. Christ institutes the sacrament of anointing by sharing with his disciples his own love and solicitude for the sick and suffering. They began to fulfill this ministry even before the Lord's sacrifice on Calvary: "They drove out many demons, and they anointed with oil many who were sick and cured them" (Mark 6:13). Soon after Pentecost, Peter inaugurated the Church's mission of healing in Christ's name when he said to the man born crippled: "I have neither silver nor gold, but what I do have I give you: in the name of Jesus Christ the Nazorean, (rise and) walk" (Acts 3:6). Before long, Peter and the apostles had developed a reputation for healing that resembled the reputation that Jesus had before them (Acts 5:16).

Just as Christ told the apostles to care for the sick, they passed on this charge to the priests of the Church. James the Apostle writes:

> Is anyone among you sick? He should summon the presbyters of the church, and they should pray over him and anoint (him) with oil in the name of the Lord, and the prayer of faith will save the sick person, and the Lord will raise him up. If he has committed any sins, he will be forgiven (James 5:14–15).

Here, James indicates that the ministers of the sacrament of anointing are presbyters. The Greek word, *presbyteroi*, and its Latin equivalent, *presbyteri*, often are translated into English as "priests." When he writes of "the presbyters of the church," James refers "to that specific category of the faithful who, through the imposition of hands, the Holy Spirit had ordained to tend the Church of God" (NM). This is the constant interpretation and practice of the Church, received from Christ and passed on by the apostles. Christ instituted the sacrament of anointing such that only priests and bishops can serve as its ministers. As a result, this is part of the essential rite that the Church has no power to change.

Some confusion has arisen in recent years about deacons and laity who serve as chaplains in hospitals. Priests sometimes are unavailable in hospitals or in other places where sick or dying Catholics are found. This has led some to wonder why deacons and lay ministers are not able to anoint the sick. Once again, the divine institution of the sacrament of anointing—promulgated through the Apostle James and consistently practiced by the Church—established beyond a doubt that only priests and bishops can serve as ministers of this sacrament. A lay person or deacon cannot administer the sacrament of anointing. If one attempts to administer the sacrament of anointing of the sick, or gives the false impression of administering that sacrament, he or she is guilty of a grave sin called "simulation of a sacrament."

The priestly prerogative to minister the sacrament of anointing stems in part from the sacrament's association with penance and the forgiveness of sins. As with the sacrament of reconciliation and the Eucharist, the priest acts *in persona Christi capitis*—that is, in the person of Christ the Head of the Church—when anointing. By virtue of his ordination, the priest represents and makes Christ present in a particular way. The priest also represents the Church before God, interceding on behalf of the Church for those who are in danger from serious illness or old age, and for their families.

During his ministry on earth, Christ exercised divine power to heal the body of physical ailments and the soul of sin. He passed this power on to bishops and priests of the Church by entrusting to them the ministry of the sacrament of anointing of the sick. Moreover, anointing is closely associated with the forgiveness of sin, which God imparts in the sacrament of penance. It is no coincidence that only a bishop or priest can minister these two sacraments. Having dealt with the minister, let us now consider the matter and form of the sacrament of anointing the sick.

"THROUGH THIS HOLY ANOINTING...": THE MATTER AND FORM

The passage from the Epistle of James quoted above sets forth the matter or physical element of the sacrament of anointing of the sick: oil. The Church traditionally uses olive oil, although Pope Paul VI allowed for the use of other vegetable (but not mineral) oils where necessary (SU). This oil is blessed by the bishop during Holy Week each year. A priest also may consecrate the oil if necessary. The general association of the oils used for anointing the sick with the bishop highlights the connection between the bishop's office and the grace of the Holy Spirit. The visible anointing of the sick Christian's body with oil symbolizes and effects an invisible anointing of the soul with the grace of the Holy Spirit.

James indicates that the presbyters "should pray over" the sick, but he does not indicate the words or form of the prayer. Therefore various liturgical traditions apply the oil with different formulas. In the extraordinary form, the priest utters the following words while anointing the eyes, ears, nose, mouth, hands, and feet:

> Through this holy anointing and through His tender mercy may the Lord forgive you whatever sins you have committed through sight...hearing...smell...taste and power of speech...touch...power of walking. (see RR 35)

The ordinary form of the Roman Rite has been simplified so that the sick or dying Christian is anointed only on the forehead and hands with the following form uttered once:

> Through this holy anointing may the Lord in his love and mercy help you with the grace of the Holy Spirit. May the Lord who frees you from sin save you and raise you up. (PS 124)

The priest may anoint additional parts of the body, but without repeating the sacramental form.

The formulas used for the ordinary and extraordinary forms highlight the forgiveness that Christ grants through the sacrament of anointing. Expressions in the rite of anointing such as "May the Lord...raise you up" are intentionally ambiguous. They leave open the possibility that the Lord might heal the illness of the recipient while forgiving his or her sins. Since these words indicate the invisible grace of the anointing of the sick, they naturally lead to a consideration of the sacrament's effects.

EFFECTS OF THE SACRAMENT OF ANOINTING

As we saw in the chapter on confirmation, oil symbolizes the gift of the Holy Spirit. The same observation pertains to the sacrament of anointing of the sick. This invisible grace brings about three, and possibly four, categories of effects: comfort and strength, union with Christ and the Church, remission of sins, and actual healing of the sickness itself.

Comfort and Strength. The sacrament of anointing comforts and strengthens the soul of the sick or dying Christian. Through this sacrament, the Lord imparts peace to the suffering soul by bolstering confidence in divine mercy and strengthening it in virtue. Bolstered with such supernatural comfort, the afflicted Christian more willingly bears the sufferings of sickness or old age. The sacrament of anointing also infuses the suffering Christian with divine strength to more effectively resist the temptations of the devil. The moment of death is the devil's last opportunity to attempt to secure the soul's damnation, and so the devil is particularly active at this time. Thus the dying soul greatly needs the strength to resist temptation and to persevere in faith, hope, and charity to the end.

Union with Christ. The sacrament of anointing of the sick also strengthens the suffering Christian's union with Christ and the Church. The sacrament helps the stricken Christian realize the redemptive value of Christian suffering by joining his or her suffering to that of Christ on the cross (see Isaiah 53:11). When a Christian joins his or her suffering with the sacrifice of Christ, the suffering takes on saving significance. The sacrament of anointing "unites the sick with Christ's self-offering for the salvation of all, so that they too, within the mystery of the communion of saints, can participate in the redemption of the world" (SCar 22). From this perspective, anointing completes the union with Christ's passion that begins with baptism into his death and that is consummated by eucharistic participation in his sacrifice.

Forgiveness. The third effect of the sacrament of anointing of the sick is the forgiveness of sins. The Holy Spirit remits or pardons sin if any remains in the sick or dying Christian. From this perspective, the sacramental anointing acts on the soul wounded by sin as a healing remedy. Anointing is a spiritual medicine, a balm or salve for the soul. If repentance occurs while a patient is still conscious but is unable to approach the sacrament of penance, then the sacrament of anointing forgives mortal sins as well. The Christian near death is in vital need of divine forgiveness, since he or she is approaching the moment of personal judgment.

Physical Healing. The anointing of the sick may bring about a physical healing of the body as well as the soul. This, however, is not a benefit offered infallibly or necessarily through the sacrament. If it is expedient or helpful for the soul of the recipient, then the Lord may heal his or her physical illness. Why the sacrament of anointing should lead to physical healings in some instances and not in others is a mystery hidden in the will of God.

PREPARING FOR OUR HEAVENLY HOMELAND: THE RECIPIENT OF ANOINTING

Who should receive the sacrament of anointing of the sick, and how can he or she best participate in it? In order to validly receive the sacrament of anointing, the recipient must meet several criteria.

The recipient must be a baptized Christian who has attained the age of reason, and who is in danger due to illness, injury, or old age. A priest should administer anointing if there is any doubt about whether the Christian has attained the use of reason or is in a dangerous condition (*CCL* 1004–1005).

The recipient must be a baptized Christian preparing for a serious operation, or be an elderly, sick, or injured individual whose condition remarkably worsens. The common cold or other minor ailments and injuries are insufficient grounds for receiving this sacramental anointing.

Only a living Christian validly receives the anointing of the sick. If a priest is uncertain about whether someone is dead, he should administer anointing to that person. Someone who is undoubtedly dead, however, cannot validly receive the sacrament.

The Second Vatican Council ensured that anointing of the sick was not reserved solely for those at the point of death: "as soon as any one of the faithful begins to be in danger of death from sickness or old age, the fitting time for him to receive this sacrament has certainly already arrived" (SC 73). Therefore the council preferred "anointing of the sick" to "extreme unction" as a title for this sacrament. Extreme unction—or final anointing—has a grim connotation for some who fear that receiving it means death is imminent.

In order to fruitfully receive anointing of the sick, a conscious recipient also must be in a state of grace. One who is unconscious should have repented of grave sin before becoming unconscious. The recipient also should be resigned to the will of God and desire to be united with God. An unrepentant Christian who obstinately persists in manifest serious sin may not receive anointing of the sick.

Anointing of the sick can be administered in a home, in a hospital, at an accident site, or any place where the need is obvious. Priests also may offer anointing within the context of a Mass offered for the sick and aged. The sacrament of reconciliation and holy Communion constitute excellent means of preparing for anointing.

For someone who is conscious, anointing of the sick does not offer the forgiveness of mortal sin that Christ extends in the sacrament of penance. The Church offers a continuous rite for administering penance, anointing, and *Viaticum* in succession. *Viaticum* is reception of the Eucharist for the journey or the passage to eternal life. Penance, anointing of the sick, and *Viaticum* together constitute "the sacraments that prepare for our heavenly homeland" or "the sacraments that complete the earthly pilgrimage" (*CCC* 1524–1525). They are received when the struggle of the Christian life on earth is nearly over. The time of trial and pilgrimage, and watching and waiting draws to a close as the Christian longs for heaven and courageously awaits the mercy of God. Penance, anointing, and the Eucharist together seal the life of the Christian on earth, and provide final fortification with sacramental grace before approaching the merciful but strict judgment of Christ.

The sacraments that prepare for our heavenly homeland draw to a conclusion the life of grace in God's mercy and forgiveness that began at baptism. Baptism is the first sacrament whereby sin is wiped away, and with baptism the Christian life begins. Penance is the sacrament for those struggling against sin and temptation in order to live the life of grace in accordance with the Gospel. With penance, the Lord restores the life of sanctifying grace to one who has lost it through sin but who subsequently repented and sought forgiveness. Especially for a recipient who is near death, the sacrament of anointing of the sick brings both baptism and penance to completion (*CT* 14). The final reception of holy Communion provides food for the journey to eternal life. The Christian who dies having fruitfully participated in these sacraments will praise God in heaven, participating in eternal divine worship with the angels and saints forever.

DISCUSSION QUESTIONS

1. *In what sense is Christ "the physician?"*

2. *What is the relationship between the healing of sin and the healing of sickness?*

3. *How is anointing of the sick related to other sacraments?*

4. *Who can and who cannot receive the anointing of the sick?*

5. *Who can and who cannot serve as the minister of anointing?*

ABBREVIATIONS AND SOURCES

CCC: *Catechism of the Catholic Church.* 1499–1532.

CCL: *Code of Canon Law.* Canons. Canons 998–1007.

CT 14: Council of Trent, Session 14. The Doctrine of the Sacrament of Extreme Unction. November 25, 1551.

NM: Congregation for the Doctrine of the Faith. Note on the Minister of the Sacrament of the Anointing of the Sick, with accompanying letter and commentary. February 11, 2005.

PS: Pastoral Care of the Sick: Rites of Anointing and Viaticum. *In The Rites of the Catholic Church*, vol. 1, pp. 761-908. Collegeville, MN: Liturgical Press, 1990.

RR: *The Roman Ritual: In Latin and English With Rubrics and Planechant Notation*, vol. 1, *The Sacraments and Sacramentals.* Trans. and ed. Philip T. Weller. Milwaukee: Bruce, 1950. The modern language rendition shown in the text for the "extraordinary form" of the Roman rite for anointing of the sick is based on the version in this source, which uses archaic terms such as "thee" and "thou."

SC: Constitution on the Sacred Liturgy *Sacrosanctum Concilium.* December 4, 1963.

SCar: Pope Benedict XVI. Post-Synodal Apostolic Exhortation on the Eucharist as the Source and Summit of the Church's Life and Mission *Sacramentum Caritatis.* February 22, 2007.

SU: Pope Paul VI. Apostolic Constitution on the Sacrament of Anointing of the Sick *Sacram Unctionem Infirmorum.* November 30, 1972.

FOR FURTHER READING

Pope John Paul II. Apostolic Letter on the Christian Meaning of Human Suffering *Salvifici Doloris.* February 11, 1984.

CHAPTER 7

Holy Orders
Consecrated to Serve

The final two sacraments, holy orders and matrimony, are called sacraments at the service of communion because they serve to build up the communion of the Church. The Lord instituted the sacraments of holy orders and matrimony not only for the salvation of individual recipients, but also for the salvation of others. Through baptism and confirmation, all Catholics have a share in the priesthood and mission of Christ to build up the Church and to evangelize the world. Through holy orders and marriage, God specifies the initiated Christians' sharing in Christ's action by consecrating the recipients for a particular mission within the Church. These missions are especially aimed at building up the people of God.

This chapter explores the first of the sacraments at the service of communion, holy orders. Despite the plural name, holy orders is only one sacrament. The orders indicates that the sacrament includes several grades or steps: the diaconate (deacons), the presbyterate (priests or presbyters), and the episcopate (bishops).

Beginning with the diaconate, ordination to each of these orders or grades constitutes a fuller participation in the one priesthood of

Jesus Christ. The Catholic Church in English-speaking locations tends to translate to the Latin word *presbyter* as "priest" rather than "presbyter." The Latin word for an ordained priest, however, is *sacerdos*, and it can be used to indicate either a presbyter (*presbyter*) or a bishop (*episcopus*). This Latin terminology reflects the fact that both presbyters and bishops act as priests—especially when they offer the divine sacrifice of the Eucharist. Yet bishops are of a higher order than presbyters. Bishops possess what in Latin is called the *summum sacerdotium*, the "high priesthood" (LG 21).

Because the ordained have a unique participation in the one priesthood of Christ, our treatment of holy orders will begin with Christ's priesthood. Then we will explore the divine institution of the sacrament of holy orders, along with its essential rite and effects. With regard to the rite and the effects, distinctions must be made between the three grades of holy orders: diaconate, presbyterate, and episcopate. Finally, we will define several significant terms: major orders, minor orders, and ministries.

CHRIST THE HIGH PRIEST

From the first chapter of this book, liturgy has been framed in terms of the action of Christ the High Priest. Christ institutes the sacraments and they are efficacious by virtue of his passion, death, resurrection, and ascension. Any sacramental action of the Church is a participation in the priesthood of Christ. The recipient of holy orders participates in Christ's priesthood in a particular manner and to a degree that is greater than the participation of the lay or nonordained faithful in Christ's priesthood.

The priesthood of the old covenant was hereditary. The Lord chose the men who belonged to the tribe of Levi and in a particular way from the family of Moses' brother Aaron to offer the Israelites' sacrifices before God. Aaron's sons and the men of the tribe of Levi ministered to the Lord first at the Tabernacle in the desert and later at the great Temple Solomon built in Jerusalem. Those who did not belong to these hereditary lines could not serve as priests under the old covenant. Yet Jesus was not a descendant of Aaron or Levi. He belonged to the family of David and the tribe of Judah. How, then, could Christ be the definitive high priest of Israel? Christ's priesthood stems from another line that predates the lives of Aaron, Levi, and their children—the line of Melchizedek.

Psalm 110 prophesied that the Messiah would be an eternal priest like Melchizedek: "The LORD has sworn and will not waver: 'Like Melchizedek,'" or according to the order of Melchizedek, "'you are a priest forever'" (Psalm 110:4). In the Gospels, Christ applies this Psalm to himself (Matthew 22:44, Mark 12:36, Luke 20:42–43). As the Messiah, Christ fulfills the Psalm's prophecy—his priesthood does not belong not to the line of Aaron or Levi, but belongs instead to that of Melchizedek. The Epistle to the Hebrews explains that Melchizedek is greater than Abraham and all his descendants, including Aaron and Levi:

> This "Melchizedek, king of Salem and priest of God Most High," "met Abraham as he returned from his defeat of the kings" and "blessed him." And Abraham apportioned to him "a tenth of everything." His name first means righteous king, and he was also "king of Salem," that is, king of peace. Without father, mother, or ancestry, without beginning of days or end of life, thus made to resemble the Son of God, he remains a priest forever. See how great he is to whom the patriarch "Abraham (indeed) gave a tenth" of his spoils. The descendants of Levi who receive the office of priesthood have a commandment according to the law to exact tithes from the people, that is, from their brothers, although they also have come from the loins of Abraham. But he who was not of their ancestry received tithes from Abraham and blessed

him who had received the promises. Unquestionably, a lesser person is blessed by a greater (Hebrews 7:1–7).

Thus Hebrews retells the brief account of Abraham's encounter with Melchizedek, "priest of God Most High," from the Book of Genesis (14:17–20). Hebrews argues that the priesthood of Melchizedek is greater than that of Aaron and Levi because Abraham, the ancestor of Aaron and Levi, paid a tithe to Melchizedek and was blessed by him. Among the peculiarities of Melchizedek's priesthood is the fact that he offered bread and wine in sacrifice rather than animals. Melchizedek, then, sets the pattern for the priesthood of Christ. His priesthood is not dependent on the lineage of Aaron and Levi—it is eternal, and bread and wine are at the heart of its sacrificial offering.

Christ's priesthood, then, derives from the order of Melchizedek. Therefore it is eternal and greater than the priesthood of Aaron and the priesthood of Levi. The following section explains how Christ instituted the priesthood of the new covenant as a share in his own eternal role as High Priest.

INSTITUTION OF THE PRIESTHOOD OF THE NEW COVENANT

Sacrifice and priesthood are always united. A sacrifice demands a priest to offer it, and a priest's role is to offer sacrifice. Furthermore, there can be no acceptable offering without a priest whose ministry is instituted by God. This was true of the old covenant and it is true of the new covenant in Christ's blood. The consummate act of Christ's priesthood is his offering of himself on the cross, which fulfills all the sacrifices of the old covenant, and constitutes the sacrifice of the new covenant. Christ wills his one perfect sacrifice on the cross, the source of all grace and salvation, to be continually renewed in the Eucharist so that individuals may benefit from it. To ensure the continuation of his sacrifice, our Lord instituted a priesthood to offer it.

At the same time that Christ instituted the visible sacrifice of the new covenant, the Eucharist, Christ also instituted a new and visible priesthood of the new covenant. This took place at the Last Supper, which the Church commemorates on Holy Thursday. When our Lord commanded the apostles to "do this in remembrance of me" (Luke 22:19; see 1 Corinthians 11:24), he established both the Eucharist and the priesthood. With these words, Christ enjoined upon his apostles the privilege and the duty to carry on his priesthood by continually offering the Most Holy Sacrifice. Holy Thursday, then, is the anniversary of the institution of both the Eucharist and the priesthood. This is why bishops, whenever possible, consecrate the oils used in the rite of ordination at the Chrism Mass on Holy Thursday.

Christ's institution of the ordained priesthood also is evident in the words cited earlier regarding the sacrament of reconciliation: "he breathed on them and said to them, 'Receive the holy Spirit. Whose sins you forgive are forgiven them, and whose sins you retain are retained'" (John 20:22–23). Through this mysterious gesture of breathing, the resurrected Christ confers upon the disciples the power to forgive sins. Recall that mortal and venial sins are forgiven through the sacrament of penance, while the divine sacrifice of the Mass and the anointing of the sick also offer the forgiveness of sins, though in a different manner. Only a priest can minister these three sacraments. They all are connected with the power to forgive sins that Christ entrusted to the apostles and their successors, the priests of the Church.

The conferral of the power of the Holy Spirit to remit sins through the breath of Christ occurred only once, as did the Last Supper. The apostles designated and consecrated their successors, and passed on the power of holy orders through the imposition of hands. This is evident in the New Testament, when Paul writes to Timothy: "Do not neglect the gift you have, which was conferred on you through the prophetic word with the imposition of hands of the presbyterate" (1 Timothy 4:14; see also 5:22). This apostolic succession, marked by the laying on of hands, continues in the Church today and will continue until the end of time.

In conclusion, Christ entrusted a twofold priestly power to the apostles and to their successors. First, he endowed them with the power to consecrate, offer, and minister his Body and Blood. Priests above all act *in persona Christi capitis*, or in the person of Christ the head of the Church, when they offer the eucharistic sacrifice of his Body and Blood. Second, Christ also instituted the priesthood to extend in time the forgiveness of sins that he merited through his passion, death, resurrection, and ascension. Priests extend Christ's forgiveness of sins through the sacraments of penance and anointing of the sick, as well as by offering the Mass. Let us now consider the elements of the essential rite by which men are ordained to the sacred priesthood that Christ endows with such saving powers.

ESSENTIAL RITE

The seeds of the essential rite of the sacrament of holy orders are evident in 1 Timothy. From that scriptural foundation, one can elaborate the matter, form, recipient, and minister of holy orders.

Saint Paul's letters to Timothy reveal both the matter and the minister of the sacrament of holy orders. The matter, as seen above, is the imposition of or laying-on of hands. Hence, Paul reminds Timothy of "the gift of God that you have through the imposition of my hands" (2 Timothy 1:6). Since Saint Paul is an apostle, he demonstrates by example the apostles' authority to appoint leaders of churches as their successors. Therefore the ministers of the sacrament of holy orders are bishops to whom the apostles have passed on their ministry. The bishop who ordains must himself have been ordained in a line of apostolic succession that can be traced back to Christ's breathing of the gift of the Holy Spirit upon the disciples after his resurrection. This is what the Church means by "apostolic succession." Each validly ordained bishop was ordained by another validly ordained bishop in a line of succession that traces back to one of the apostles.

How is the rite of ordination conducted today? The bishop serving as minister imposes his hands on the heads of the *ordinandi* (those to be ordained) in silence. Such is the matter of the sacrament of holy orders. The words of the preface or consecratory prayer, which are intoned after the laying on of hands, constitute the form of the sacrament. The consecratory prayer differs for each distinct step or grade of holy orders—bishop, priest, and deacon. With the consecratory prayer, the minister beseeches the outpouring of the Holy Spirit and the gifts proper to the ministry to which the candidate is being ordained.

Pope Paul VI specified the form or the words that are required for validity in each of the consecratory prayers in his apostolic constitution *Pontificalis Romani*. Here are the words required for the ordination of deacons:

Lord, send forth upon them the Holy Spirit, that they may be strengthened by the gift of your sevenfold grace to carry out the work of the ministry. (ODP 18)

The following words are prayed for the ordination of presbyters:

Almighty Father, grant to these servants of yours the dignity of the priesthood. Renew within them the Spirit of holiness. As co-workers with the order of bishops, may they be faithful to the ministry that they received from you, Lord God, and be to others a model of right conduct. (ODP 26)

The words required for the ordination of a bishop are:

> So now pour out upon this chosen one that power which is from you, the governing Spirit whom you gave to your beloved Son, Jesus Christ, the Spirit given by him to the holy apostles, who founded the Church in every place to be your temple for the unceasing glory and praise of your name. (OB 26)

The prayer for the ordination of a bishop invokes the governing spirit upon the newly ordained; the prayer for a presbyter, the spirit of counsel; and the prayer for a deacon, the spirit of zeal and solicitude.

The handing over of the instruments that symbolize each order has always been considered a significant element of ordination rites. The ordaining bishop presents the deacon with a stole and an alb or dalmatic at his ordination. To priests, the ordaining bishop hands over a stole and chasuble, and to bishops he gives a ring and pastoral staff or crozier. Although important, the handing over of the instruments is not part of the essential rite of the sacrament of holy orders (SO; PR). Nor is the consent, call, or authority of the faithful or any civil power essential to the sacrament (CT 23).

The sole valid recipient of the sacrament of holy orders is a baptized and confirmed male. After centuries of being almost entirely unquestioned, the reservation of priestly ordination to men alone has attracted much controversy in recent decades. The reason why the Church ordains only men is that Christ instituted the sacrament that way, and the Church has no power to change what the Lord has established. The practice of the Church from East and West, and throughout the centuries, bears witness to the fact that the reservation of holy orders to men is an apostolic tradition. Moreover, this matter is infallibly taught by the ordinary and universal living magisterium of the Church, and therefore it is to be definitively held by all the Church's faithful (OS 4).

No amount of discussion or argument could ever bring about a valid ordination of women. Their exclusion from the priesthood does not mean that women are of lesser dignity, nor should it be construed as discrimination against them. Saints, within whose ranks women are strongly represented, rather than ordained ministers, are the greatest in the kingdom of heaven (OS 3).

Extensive preparation, which usually takes place in a seminary, is generally required of the candidate for priesthood. In the sixteenth century, the Council of Trent mandated the establishment of seminaries for the proper training of future priests. Before that, priestly training was haphazard and differed greatly from one location to the next. The Second Vatican Council's Decree on Priestly Training *Optatam Totius* sought renewal of seminary training in the twentieth century, and set the pattern for contemporary programs of priestly formation in seminaries. Anyone desiring more details regarding the programs in seminaries should consult the latest edition of the *Program of Priestly Formation* published by the United States Conference of Catholic Bishops. The formation of future priests is so crucial to the life of the Church that a great deal of resources and energy are justifiably put into seminaries.

Let us review the elements of the essential rite of the sacrament of holy orders. The minister is a bishop validly ordained in apostolic succession. The recipient is an adult male Christian who has been called by God to the ordained ministry, and who is properly trained, usually within a seminary. The matter is the laying on of the minister's hands. The form, which differs for each of the three orders, is a specific formula found within the consecratory prayer of the rite of ordination.

CONSECRATION TO SACRED MINISTRY: THE EFFECTS OF ORDINATION

The effects of the sacrament of holy orders can be divided into two categories: the character and the grace of the Holy Spirit. Then distinctions must be made among the graces conferred through ordination to the diaconate, the presbyterate, and the episcopate.

Like baptism and confirmation, the sacrament of holy orders confers an indelible, permanent character on the soul. Therefore deacons, priests, and bishops can be ordained only once. This means that the power of the priests of the new covenant is not temporary (CT 23). Christ himself has permanently consecrated the ordained priest for the service of his Church. Therefore a person who is validly ordained cannot again become a layman. Someone who is ordained, however, may be deprived of the faculty, or discharged from the obligation, to exercise his ministry.

The sacrament of holy orders also resembles baptism and confirmation insofar as the character disposes one for the worship of God. This is particularly evident in priestly ordination, since the priest can do something no one else can do: offer the Most Holy Sacrifice of the Mass. Holy orders confers a gift of the Holy Spirit, which permits the exercise of sacred power—a power to more perfectly participate in Christ's role as priest within the Church.

The ministerial priesthood of ordained bishops and priests differs both in essence and in degree from the common priesthood of the baptized (LG 10). The ministerial priesthood is rooted in the apostolic succession, and is vested with the sacred power to act *in persona Christi*. Yet the ministerial priesthood exists fundamentally as a service to the common priesthood, a necessary aid established by God to assist the faithful on their pilgrimage to heaven. Moreover, the service of the ministerial priesthood is necessary and irreplaceable. The Church cannot exist without it. This is not to deny any similarity between the common or baptismal priesthood of the faithful and the ministerial priesthood of the ordained. Both are sustained by an indelible character, and both are a participation in the priesthood of Christ, the definitive High Priest of the new covenant. Deriving as they do from the same source, they also tend toward the same end: the perfect worship of God.

The proper grace of the sacrament of holy orders is a configuration of the recipient to Christ as priest, prophet or teacher, and king or pastor. Such grace renders ordained ministers servants of Christ and servants of the Church. They build up the Church through administration of the sacraments, authoritative proclamation of the word of God, and pastoral care. Let us consider the specifics of each order in turn, and how the ordained fulfill their share of Christ's threefold office as priest, prophet, and pastor.

DEACONS

According to the Second Vatican Council, deacons occupy a lower level of the hierarchy. At their ordination, deacons receive the imposition of hands "not unto the priesthood, but unto a ministry of service" (LG 29). Thus the deacon is not empowered to act *in persona Christi*. Rather, ordination to the diaconate configures the ordained to Christ as the deacon or servant of all.

The grace of the diaconate is a grace of service of the liturgy, the Gospel, and charity (*CCC* 1588). To deacons, the Church entrusts a number of particular roles that fall under the categories of liturgy, word, and charity. Within the liturgy, deacons can administer baptism, serve as ministers of holy Communion, assist at and bless marriages, bring *Viaticum* to the dying, read Scripture to the faithful, instruct and exhort, officiate at funeral and burial services, and conduct blessings.

Deacons cannot, however, serve as ministers of the sacraments of confirmation, reconciliation, anointing of the sick, or holy orders.

Nor can deacons act as ministers of the Eucharist. They are ministers of holy Communion but not ministers who can offer the Most Holy Sacrifice of the Mass. Outside the liturgy, deacons assume important roles in various ministries of charity and pastoral governance, according to the judgment of the local bishop and pastors.

For many centuries, the only deacons in the Roman Rite were "transitional" deacons, who were preparing for ordination to the priesthood. The Second Vatican Council allowed for restoring the permanent diaconate, even to married men, wherever local bishops thought they might be useful (LG 29). Today, some dioceses boast many permanent deacons, whereas others have none at all.

BISHOP

Let us turn from deacons at the lowest level of the hierarchy to bishops at the highest. Through episcopal ordination, God grants the bishop the fullness of the sacrament of orders, the supreme power of sacred ministry (LG 21). This fullness includes three main duties or offices, and the grace to fulfill them: teaching, sanctifying, and governing.

First is the teaching office—the responsibility for preaching the Gospel. Second is the sacramental office. Christ especially charges the bishop with responsibility for the Eucharist, as he charged the apostles with the same responsibility on Holy Thursday. Moreover, bishops are responsible for the dispensation of the sacraments throughout their dioceses. Bishops also serve as ministers of all the sacraments, with the exception of matrimony. The bishop's third and final duty is the pastoral office or the office of governance. In fulfillment of this office, bishops govern Christ's Church on earth as his vicars. God grants this office and the obligation to exercise it with a grace of strength to guide and defend the Church.

No bishop stands alone. Each bishop exercises his sacred ministry within the "college" of bishops. That means that bishops act authoritatively when they act in communion with all other bishops of the world, with the pope as their head. Although each bishop is responsible primarily for care of a particular local church, he also bears within the college of bishops a certain solicitude for all local churches or dioceses throughout the world.

PRIESTS (PRESBYTERS)

Presbyters, or priests, work with the bishop and share in the bishop's teaching, sacramental, and pastoral office. Priests share in the universal mission that Christ entrusted to the apostles and their successors. Priests must exercise their ministry in dependence on and in communion with the bishop (*CCC* 1567). United with the bishop in priestly dignity, priests are consecrated to preach the Gospel, shepherd the faithful, and celebrate divine worship (*CCC* 1562).

Ordination to the presbyterate configures the recipient to Christ the High Priest to such an extent that the ordained priest is able to act *in persona Christi*. This is especially achieved in celebration of the Eucharist, the moment when priests exercise their sacred office in a supreme degree. In addition to the sacrament of the Eucharist, priests also serve as ministers of baptism, confirmation, penance, and anointing of the sick.

MAJOR ORDERS, MINOR ORDERS, AND MINISTRIES

Before the Second Vatican Council, the Roman Church had seven orders, or ecclesiastical steps or grades. These seven orders can still be found in communities dedicated to the extraordinary form of the Roman Rite. Four of these orders are "minor": porter, lector, exorcist, and acolyte. Although not found as such in sacred Scripture, these orders arose by the third century. In subsequent centuries, the minor orders served as the primary vehicle for preparing men and testing their suitability for ordination to the major orders. The three "major" or sacred orders of the extraordinary form today (and the Roman Rite before the Second Vatican Council) are subdeacon, deacon, and priest. From this perspective, the office of bishop constitutes a higher degree of the one priesthood rather than a distinct order.

With the Second Vatican Council, the episcopate came to be seen clearly as a distinct order in its own right (LG 20–21). Following the council, Pope Paul VI changed the system of minor and major orders. He reduced the seven orders to three: deacon, priest, and bishop. Paul VI divided the roles of the subdeacon between the reader or lector and the acolyte, and reduced their status to that of "ministry" rather than "holy order."

Thus lector and acolyte become ministries conferred permanently by institution rather than minor orders conferred by ordination (MQ). While the lector proclaims the word of God (although not the Gospel) in the liturgical assembly, the acolyte aids the deacon and ministers to the priest or bishop during liturgical celebrations. Paul VI hoped to open the ministries of lector and acolyte to the laity, although in practice only those studying for ordination typically receive the institutions. This is largely owing to the fact that men alone can be permanently instituted as lectors and acolytes.

The Roman Rite also provides blessings for lay people who perform various services at liturgical celebrations, including altar servers, musicians, and sacristans. In order to properly distinguish them from the roles of the ordained, such services should not be called "ministries." In cooperation with their pastors, the non-ordained faithful may fulfill only some of the roles that properly belong to the ordained, and only to a limited degree.

An excellent example of these functions is the distribution of holy Communion. Lay people who distribute holy Communion are considered "extraordinary ministers of holy Communion" because they should distribute holy Communion only in extreme circumstances. Such circumstances occur when the numbers of faithful who receive holy Communion cannot be served adequately by a small number of deacons, priests, and bishops—that is, ordinary ministers of holy Communion (ICQ). Rather than being permanently instituted, extraordinary ministers of holy Communion are provided with a temporary commission that expires after a specified time.

To summarize, according to the older practice of holy orders, there are four minor and three major orders. Going from lowest to highest in the order that they were typically received, these orders are: porter, lector, exorcist, acolyte, subdeacon, deacon, and priest. Today, the Church considers the sacrament to consist of three major orders: deacon, priest (presbyter), and bishop. Pope Paul VI divided the roles of the lector, acolyte, and subdeacon into two ministries in which lay men can be permanently instituted—lectors and acolytes. When necessary, lay people may fulfill other liturgical functions that properly belong to the ordained. Yet Christ's lay faithful cannot live the sacramental life of the Church without ordained ministers.

VOCATIONS TO THE PRIESTHOOD

Because the priesthood is necessary for the life of the Church, continuous, zealous, and well-organized pastoral promotion of vocations is necessary. Any other solution to problems deriving from a shortage of sacred ministers can only be partial or lead to precarious consequences. Many observers today comment about the crisis of vocations. This problem is not universal, and it does not affect the priesthood alone.

Vocations to marriage and family life also are in crisis, as are vocations to the religious life. In fact, one might assert a broad crisis in the very Christian life itself, or in any pattern of life based upon charity, service, and generosity, as opposed to the pursuit of the pleasures and triumphs of the world. The only authentic solution to the Church's vocational crisis entails recourse to the sacraments and to prayer, and the personal conversion of the faithful to Christ—the *metanoia* discussed in the chapter on penance. An individual already in holy orders or who is preparing for holy orders especially is called to conversion before the grandeur and dignity of the priestly office to which Christ has called him (*CCC* 1550, 1589).

CONCLUSION

Beginning with Christ's role as the High Priest of the New Covenant, we have explored the sacrament of holy orders as participation in Christ's priesthood. At the Last Supper, Christ instituted the priesthood of the new covenant at the same time as the Most Holy Sacrifice of the Eucharist, to which that priesthood would be dedicated. Christ also entrusted the ordained priesthood with the power to forgive sins, which is exercised through the administration of several sacraments. Holy orders include three distinct grades, with each participating in the fullness of Christ's priesthood in a different way: deacon, priest or presbyter, and bishop.

Bishops possess the fullest share in Christ's priesthood. Together with the bishops, priests are needed for the administration of the sacraments of the Eucharist, confirmation, penance, anointing of the sick, and holy orders. The sacrament of holy orders is conferred by the bishop through the laying on of hands, and accompanied by the words of the consecratory prayer. The recipient of the sacrament of holy orders receives a character and a special grace that conforms that individual to Christ's threefold office as priest, teacher, and pastor.

With this sacramental consecration, the recipient of holy orders is dedicated to the service of the Church. In fact, holy orders is vital to the life of the Church. Therefore the faithful should work and pray to promote vocations to the ordained life of service to the Church. We also should work and pray that couples will approach the sacrament of matrimony and live according to the married vocation in faith, hope, and charity. To this second sacrament at the service of communion we now turn our attention.

DISCUSSION QUESTIONS

1. *How many orders are there, and what are the differences between them?*

2. *When and how did Christ institute the sacrament of holy orders?*

3. *Within the sphere of the sacraments, what can deacons do, and what are they not able to do?*

4. *What is the matter and form of the sacrament of holy orders?*

5. *Who is the recipient of the sacrament of holy orders?*

6. *Why can only men be ordained?*

7. *Which sacraments confer a character on the soul?*

8. *What are the effects of the sacrament of holy orders?*

9. *Why should lay people not be called "ministers?"*

ABBREVIATIONS AND SOURCES

CCC: Catechism of the Catholic Church. 1536–1600.

CCL: Code of Canon Law. Canons 1008–1154.

CT 23: Council of Trent, Session 23. The True and Catholic Doctrine Concerning the Sacrament of Order. July 15, 1563.

ICQ: Congregation for the Clergy. Instruction on Certain Questions Regarding the Collaboration of the Non-ordained Faithful in the Sacred Ministry of Priest. August 15, 1997.

LG: Second Vatican Council. Dogmatic Constitution on the Church *Lumen Gentium.* November 21, 1964.

MQ: Pope Paul VI. Apostolic Letter Given *Motu Proprio Ministeria Quaedam.* August 15, 1972.

OB: Ordination of a Bishop. In *The Rites of the Catholic Church*, vol. 2, pp. 65–78. Collegeville, MN: Liturgical Press: 1991.

ODP: Ordination of Deacons and Priests. In *The Rites of the Catholic Church*, vol. 2, pp. 48–64. Collegeville, MN: Liturgical Press, 1991.

OS: Pope John Paul II. Apostolic Letter On Reserving Priestly Ordination to Men Alone *Ordinatio Sacerdotalis.* May 22, 1994.

PR: Pope Paul VI. Apostolic Constitution *Pontificalis Romani.* June 18, 1968.

SO: Pope Pius XII. Apostolic Constitution on the Sacrament of Order *Sacramentum Ordinis.* November 30, 1947.

FOR FURTHER READING

Fisher, John. *The Defence of the Priesthood*. Intro. Stanley L. Jaki. Trans. Philip E. Haller. Real View Books, 1996.

International Theological Commission. *From the Diakonia of Christ to the Diakonia of the Apostles*. Chicago: Hillenbrand Books, 2004.

Second Vatican Council. Decree Concerning the Pastoral Office of Bishops in the Church *Christus Dominus*. October 28, 1965.

Second Vatican Council. Decree on the Ministry and Life of Priests *Presbyterorum Ordinis*. October 28, 1965.

Second Vatican Council. Decree on Priestly Training *Optatam Totius*. October 28, 1965.

United States Conference of Catholic Bishops. *Program of Priestly Formation*. 5th ed. Washington, D.C.: United States Conference of Catholic Bishops, 2006.

CHAPTER 8

Matrimony
The Image of Divine Fidelity

The second sacrament at the service of communion is matrimony. This chapter begins by exploring God's plan for marriage as it is steadily revealed through the history of salvation. We will then examine the essential rite, focusing particularly on the minister and the recipient of the sacrament of matrimony. The subsequent section will discuss the three goods of matrimony as an institution, followed by the effects of the sacrament of matrimony. The means for fruitful participation in the sacrament of matrimony pose the next significant topic for investigation. Then this chapter will close after a brief discussion of annulments.

MARRIAGE IN GOD'S PLAN

Wedding feasts and the state of marriage are found throughout sacred Scripture, from the first chapters of Genesis to the final chapter of the Book of Revelation. This section explores just a few occurrences of matrimonial imagery within Scripture to illustrate how God gradually revealed his plan for marriage and the family.

Marriage is unique among the seven sacraments insofar as God instituted it before the Incarnation of Christ, in the Garden of Eden. Adam's first recorded words are an expression of joy in reaction to the creation of Eve: "This one, at last, is bone of my bones and flesh of my flesh" (Genesis 2:23). The author of Genesis goes on to comment: "That is why a man leaves his father and mother and clings to his wife, and the two of them become one body" (Genesis 2:24). Nonetheless, it took the ancient Israelites some time to grasp the full impact of God's will for marriage. Like the nations around them, they practiced polygamy and divorce for many centuries. Over time, God more fully revealed to the Israelites the divine plan for marriage and the family.

Much of this revelation about matrimony appears in symbolism throughout sacred Scripture. Divine revelation frequently compares the relationship between the people of Israel and the Lord with the relationship between a bride and her husband. The prophet Hosea illustrates this relationship most dramatically.

Hosea's marriage reflected the relationship between God, ever faithful to his covenant, and his people Israel, who committed adultery by worshipping false gods. Despite their infidelities, God promised that he would remain eternally faithful to his people if they repented and returned to him: "I will espouse you to me forever: I will espouse you in right and in justice, in love and in mercy" (Hosea 2:21). As we have seen, such repentance and conversion to God— such *metanoia*—underlies the sacraments of baptism and penance. Founded on conversion toward God and love of Christ, the Church is the bride (2 Corinthians 11:2; Revelation 19:7) of Christ the bridegroom (John 3:29; see also Ephesians 5:22–33).

As the time of the Incarnation drew near, God articulated his plan for matrimony more plainly: "I hate divorce, says the LORD, the God of Israel, And covering one's garment with injustice, says the LORD of hosts; You must then safeguard life that is your own, and not break faith." (Malachi 2:16)

Picking up where the prophet Malachi left off, Christ fully articulates the divine plan for marriage:

Because of the hardness of your hearts Moses allowed you to divorce your wives, but from the beginning it was not so. I say to you, whoever divorces his wife (unless the marriage is unlawful) and marries another commits adultery. (Matthew 19:8–9)

Our Lord goes on to reveal that marriage is not merely a human contract or arrangement. Marriage is a divinely established union, a perpetual and indissoluble bond: "Therefore what God has joined together, no human being must separate" (Matthew 19:6; Mark 10:9). Thus our Lord raises matrimony to the level of a sacrament of the new law.

Beginning with Genesis, God gradually revealed the divine plan for marriage in the Old Testament. Christ then raised matrimony to the level of a sacrament, emphasizing its permanent character among the baptized. Moreover, marriage possesses a deeper, symbolic meaning. Sacred Scripture uses the relationship between spouses to symbolically illustrate the relationship between the Lord and his people. Before further exploring this deeper meaning of the sacrament of matrimony, we will consider the visible sign with which it comes into being.

THE ESSENTIAL RITE: MUTUAL CONSENT OF THE SPOUSES

This section sets forth the elements of the essential rite of the sacrament of matrimony, including its ministers and recipients. Here we also will briefly consider the public character of the sacrament of matrimony. Although non-Christian couples can enter what the

Church recognizes as true marriage, our focus is on the sacrament of matrimony among the baptized.

The ministers and the recipients of the sacrament of matrimony are one and the same: the spousal couple, consisting of one baptized man and one baptized woman. As is the case with all sacraments, the ministers and recipients must meet certain conditions or prerequisites. If a marriage is to be a sacrament, both individuals must be baptized, though not necessarily Catholic.

A Catholic may marry someone who is not baptized, but their marriage is not considered a sacrament. The recipients of the sacrament of matrimony also must be free to marry. This requires that the recipients not be married already or be bound by a vow of chastity. One cannot marry a close relative either, such as a brother, sister, father, or mother. More could be said regarding such impediments to a valid marriage, but we must turn now to the heart of the sacrament of matrimony.

The mutual consent of the spouses is the heart of the sacrament of marriage; it constitutes the form of the sacrament. As ministers of the sacrament, husband and wife mutually confer upon each other the sacrament of matrimony by expressing their consent to marriage before the Church. The beginning of marriage is a deliberate and free act of the will for both individuals. To be considered an act of the will, both must have the use of reason. Obviously, free consent can be given or accepted under constraint. For example, a shotgun wedding, in which one of the parties marries under threat of death, is invalid.

The free consent that constitutes the essential rite of the sacrament of matrimony must be mutual and declared with words in the present tense. "I will take you to be my bride…." does not express a present intention, but rather a future one. It could be interpreted as a promise of marriage or engagement, rather than as consent to marry in the present. Aside from the necessity of the present tense, the

Church allows some latitude with regard to the exact formulation of the mutual consent. This latitude is found in both the ordinary and the extraordinary forms of the Roman Rite. The couple can express mutual consent with a set formula, or by providing answers to questions proposed by the one who assists.

What does it mean to "assist" at the sacrament of matrimony? We have established that, in the Roman Rite, the priest or deacon who presides over the liturgical celebration of a marriage is not the minister of the sacrament. Rather, he is said to assist at the marriage. One who assists at a marriage asks for the spouses' consent, receives it in the name of the Church, and bestows the Church's blessing upon the newly married couple. The presence of one who assists in the name of the Church is so important that it is generally necessary for the validity of the sacrament.

Two witnesses also must be present for a valid marriage in the Church (*CCL* 1108). The one who assists at a wedding—the official witness—along with the other witnesses who observe the wedding, preserve the public character of the consent in a sacramental marriage. This public character protects the mutual commitment of the spouses and helps them remain faithful to that commitment. The official witness, along with the other witnesses, also provides the Church with certainty regarding the celebration of the marriage.

In summary, the essential rite of the sacrament of matrimony is the free and mutual consent of the baptized man and baptized woman. The man and the woman are both the ministers and the recipients of the sacrament. They administer and receive the sacrament in the presence of an official witness who assists in the name of the Church, along with at least two other witnesses.

THE THREE GOODS OF MARRIAGE

God has blessed the institution of marriage with three fundamental goods: children, fidelity or conjugal love, and indissolubility. These goods are not limited to Christian marriage—they pertain to all marriages on the level of human nature. The grace of the sacrament elevates and perfects the three goods. So before considering the grace of matrimony more specifically, this section will cover each of the three goods of marriage in general.

Children are considered the greatest good or "the supreme gift" of marriage (GS 50). Through marriage, couples are called to participate or cooperate in God's act of creating new human life. Procreation is only the initial means by which marriage serves the good of children. More broadly, God has ordained marriage for the education and nourishment of children on social, physical, and spiritual levels. Parents are the first and principal educators of their children. Therefore the fruitfulness of conjugal love extends to moral, spiritual, and supernatural life that parents pass on to their children through education and by introducing them to the sacramental life of the Church. In turn, children contribute substantially to the welfare of their parents, in part by providing them with occasions to grow in Christian love and other virtues.

Fidelity as a good of marriage refers to conjugal love. Conjugal love is the mutual self-giving that is unique and exclusive to spouses. Marriage can be called the institution of conjugal love. Such love is a good from which spouses benefit, as well as a duty they owe one another. Spouses experience conjugal love as a joy and a delight. Indeed, conjugal love is one of the greatest natural joys known to human beings. The bond of matrimony is the origin of conjugal love, the bastion of its defense, and the source of its nourishment.

Conjugal love may encompass what the Church calls "the conjugal act" or "the marriage act," but conjugal love must be distinguished from the conjugal act. The conjugal act is the act of sexual intercourse between spouses. As such, it occurs only within the bond of marriage. The conjugal act, according to God's plan, includes two inseparable meanings: the unitive, which unites husband and wife with the closest of bonds; and the procreative, which leaves them open to new life (HV 12). By contrast, conjugal love is the self-sacrificing love that spouses have toward one another. It is the love that animates their lives together, and that manifests itself in mutual support and encouragement. Conjugal love endures even when the conjugal act is not possible—for example, in times of separation, injury, or illness.

Four words characterize conjugal love: human, total, exclusive, and fruitful (HV 9). Conjugal love is human insofar as it involves the entirety of both spouses in body and soul, and depends on their act of free will. Conjugal love also can be described as total because it is a special form of personal friendship whereby spouses generously share everything they are and everything they have. The strict fidelity or exclusivity of conjugal love until the end of life sometimes is difficult. But it is noble, meritorious, and possible—especially with the grace of the sacrament of matrimony. Finally, conjugal love is fruitful because it looks beyond itself to raise up new life. Since conjugal love is characteristically fruitful, there can be no contradiction between authentic conjugal love and procreation. In fact, conjugal love engenders desire for procreation and children. For this reason, the inability to have children can cause profound suffering for spouses.

> ...whatever its cause or prognosis, sterility is certainly a difficult trial. The community of believers is called to shed light upon and support the suffering of those who are unable to fulfill their legitimate aspiration to motherhood and fatherhood. Spouses who find themselves in this sad situation are called to find in it an opportunity for sharing in a particular

way in the Lord's cross, the source of spiritual fruitfulness. Sterile couples must not forget that "even when procreation is not possible, conjugal life does not for this reason lose its value. Physical sterility in fact can be for spouses the occasion for other important services to the life of the human person, for example, adoption, various forms of educational work, and assistance to other families and to poor or handicapped children." (DV 8)

Thus even for childless spouses, the fruitfulness of conjugal love manifests itself in a life of Christian charity.

Indissolubility is the third good of marriage. Indissolubility means that a marriage cannot be dissolved by either spouse. While indissolubility is a characteristic of every marriage, even among non-Christians, it is strengthened and perfected by the sacrament of marriage. Indissolubility protects conjugal love, drives away jealousy, and affords many other advantages—including stability and security—to both spouses and their children.

Each good of marriage is threatened by errors or vices that are fundamentally opposed to that good, and Christians must remain on guard against these. Errors opposed to the good of children stem from a hedonistic mentality that regards children as burdens rather than gifts. Such errors support the use of contraceptive chemicals and devices, and even the "unspeakable crimes" of abortion and infanticide (GS 51). Errors against the good of conjugal fidelity include sexual promiscuity, as well as a base notion of conjugal love that reduces it to lust. Errors against indissolubility include attacks against the indissolubility and the sacred character of marriage, along with the increasing facility of divorce. Against such errors, the principal remedies are prayer and the sacraments, docility to the teaching of the Church, grace and cooperation between spouses, and extensive preparation of couples for marriage.

The three goods of marriage—children, fidelity, and indissolubility—are elevated and reach their perfection through sacramental grace, our next topic.

INVISIBLE GRACE AND VISIBLE IMAGE OF DIVINE FIDELITY

Through the sacrament of matrimony, the Lord grants spouses graces that can be divided into three categories: the conjugal bond between husband and wife; particular graces that consecrate and strengthen spouses to fulfill their vocation to conjugal love; and participation in the bond of love and fidelity that unites Christ and the Church. This section is dedicated to exploring each of these effects.

The Conjugal Bond. According to Pope John Paul II, "the first and immediate effect of marriage (*res et sacramentum*) is not supernatural grace itself, but the Christian conjugal bond" (FC 13). God establishes this conjugal bond when he joins the spouses together in accordance with their mutual consent. The conjugal bond significantly differs from the indelible characters imparted by the sacraments of baptism, confirmation, and holy orders. These three characters cannot be erased or repeated, and so each of these three sacraments can be received only once. On the other hand, the conjugal bond dissolves with the death of one of the spouses. As a result, the living spouse may marry again.

There are, however, some similarities between the conjugal bond and the sacramental characters imprinted on the soul by baptism, confirmation, and holy orders. The matrimonial bond abides as a pledge and promise of grace oriented toward the perfection of the married Christian life. Much like the sacramental characters, the matrimonial bond also can be separated from the grace that flows from it. In other words, the Christian conjugal bond remains even when one or both spouses do not fruitfully participate in it. We will return to this topic after considering the sacramental grace that flows from the Christian conjugal bond.

Specific Graces. What specific sacramental graces flow from the Christian conjugal bond established by the sacrament of marriage? In addition to increasing the sanctifying grace received in the sacrament of baptism, the sacrament of matrimony offers graces that spouses need to fulfill the demands of the married state in Christian virtue. With the sacrament of matrimony, Christian spouses are fortified and receive a kind of consecration in the duties and dignity of their state. The grace of matrimony enables married Christians to achieve the perfection of their vocation as spouses and parents. This grace perfects the natural love of spouses and parents in Christian charity, and strengthens the couple's indissoluble unity. Furthermore, the grace of the sacrament of matrimony enables Christian spouses to help one another along the path to holiness (CCC 1641, 1661; CT 24).

Christ is the source of the grace of the sacrament of matrimony, as he is the source of grace offered in the other six sacraments. Through his passion, death, and resurrection, Christ merited the grace to perfect natural love, strengthen the indissoluble bond of Christian spouses, and sanctify them (CT 24). Saint Paul strikingly parallels spousal love with the passion of Christ in his Epistle to the Ephesians:

> Husbands, love your wives, even as Christ loved the church and handed himself over for her to sanctify her, cleansing her by the bath of water with the word, that he might present to himself the church in splendor, without spot or wrinkle or any such thing, that she might be holy and without blemish. So (also) husbands should love their wives as their own bodies. He who loves his wife loves himself. For no one hates his own flesh but rather nourishes and cherishes it, even as Christ does the church, because we are members of his body. "For this reason a man shall leave (his) father and (his) mother and be joined to his wife, and the two shall become

one flesh." This is a great mystery, but I speak in reference to Christ and the church. (Ephesians 5:25–32)

In this passage, Saint Paul roots the love of Christian spouses in the love of Christ for the Church. Christ demonstrated this selfless love above all by sacrificing himself on the cross. Christ's self-sacrifice models and makes possible the self-sacrificing love that Christian spouses should have for one another.

Here we see how deeply the marriage between a Christian man and woman participates in and is a visible sign of something still greater—the relationship between Christ and the Church. Christian marriage is an efficacious sign and image of the eternal and divine fidelity and love that Christ bears for the Church. Through the sacrament of matrimony, Christian couples "are called to participate truly in the irrevocable indissolubility that binds Christ to the Church his bride, loved by him to the end" (FC 20).

To summarize, the effects of the sacrament of matrimony may be divided into three categories. First, the sacrament brings about the Christian conjugal bond. Second, this bond is the pledge and source of graces by which Christian spouses are strengthened and consecrated to fulfill their vocations as spouses, and possibly as parents. Third, through the merits of Christ's passion, spouses' conjugal love and fidelity become an image of and a participation in Christ's love and fidelity for the Church.

PREPARATION FOR FRUITFUL PARTICIPATION

To fully benefit from the graces of the sacrament of matrimony, recipients must fruitfully participate in the sacrament. Such participation hinges on the preparation and disposition of the recipients. This section briefly considers the basic disposition for participation in the sacrament of matrimony, along with the three stages of preparation for the sacrament: remote, proximate, and immediate.

As is the case with all other sacraments, recipients benefit from matrimony to the extent that they are properly disposed to participate in it. We have learned that being in a state of grace, free from mortal sin, is necessary for fruitful participation in the sacraments of confirmation, the Eucharist, the anointing of the sick, and holy orders. This also is true of the sacrament of matrimony. The Christian conjugal bond remains even when one or both spouses are in mortal sin, and cannot benefit from the specific graces that flow from the sacrament of matrimony. Couples guilty of the sin of fornication, for example, must be forgiven through the sacrament of penance before they can fully participate in the sacrament of matrimony.

As a result, spouses must repent of former sins and turn to the Lord through the process of conversion to most fully benefit from the grace offered in the sacrament of matrimony. For this reason, the sacrament of penance constitutes an important part of preparation for the sacrament of marriage.

The opportunity for sacramental grace remains as long as the Christian conjugal bond endures. That said, spouses must continually cooperate with the conjugal bond as well. Ongoing conversion and frequent recourse to penance allow Christian spouses continually to enjoy the wealth of graces that God associates with the conjugal bond.

Preparation for marriage includes remote, proximate, and immediate preparation. Remote preparation begins in childhood, when children witness and learn about marriage by observing their parents. The local church contributes to remote preparation for marriage by forming children in Christian virtue, and by catechizing children about various issues, including sexual morality and the goods of marriage. Proximate preparation begins when a couple decides to marry, and continues as the time for marriage draws near.

On an intellectual level, the couple should recognize "that marriage is a permanent partnership between a man and a woman ordered to the procreation of offspring by means of some sexual coop-eration" (*CCL* 1096 §1). There is no such thing as perfect preparation for a sacrament, and the Church admits to matrimony those who are imperfectly disposed. But those who explicitly reject God's plan for marriage are not ready to celebrate the sacrament:

> [W]hen in spite of all efforts, engaged couples show that they reject explicitly and formally what the Church intends to do when the marriage of baptized persons is celebrated, the pastor of souls cannot admit them to the celebration of mar-riage....In these circumstances, it is not the Church that is placing an obstacle in the way of the celebration that they are asking for, but themselves (FC 68).

This is a weighty responsibility for pastors. In addition to the pastors, the local Christian community is called to share in the task of forming engaged couples for marriage through education, prayer, example, and aid. Immediate preparation takes place in the months and weeks immediately preceding the wedding. Immediate prepa-ration for fruitful reception of the sacrament of matrimony should include the sacrament of penance, as well as the frequent reception of holy Communion.

Preparation for the sacrament of matrimony is a lifelong pro-cess. Remote preparation begins during childhood, and proceeds especially through the witness of healthy sacramental marriages. Proximate preparation begins when a couple decides to marry. The local Christian community prepares the couple for marriage through various means, including education and prayer. Immediate preparation should include intense prayer, along with reception of the sacraments of penance and the Eucharist. Couples who cultivate ongoing conversion will most fully and fruitfully benefit from the graces of matrimony—both on the day the sacrament is celebrated and throughout their lives together.

ANNULMENT

The Church's teaching on the sacrament of marriage is beautiful and inspiring. Owing to the weakness of fallen human nature, however, a great number of difficulties arise to complicate matrimonial matters. Before concluding this chapter, let us consider an institution that attempts to deal with such difficulties—annulment.

A valid marriage between baptized persons that is consummated by the conjugal act cannot be dissolved by human power; it can only be dissolved by death. Our Lord taught us that "whoever divorces his wife (unless the marriage is unlawful) and marries another commits adultery" (Matthew 19:8–9). Throughout the centuries, the Catholic Church has remained faithful to the Lord's words not only when it has been convenient, but also when it has been inconvenient.

When ecclesiastical officials consider the possibility of an annulment, they ask whether a marriage is valid. Annulment is not an attempt to dissolve what God has joined. Following rigorous investigation, it is a statement essentially asserting that what looked like a marriage was not, in fact, a marriage. Certain factors can so compromise, for example, the integrity of mutual consent, as to render a marriage invalid.

If someone enters into a marriage under false pretenses and is willfully deceived in order to gain consent, the marriage is not considered valid. Similarly, a marriage is considered invalid if a spouse is forced or coerced into the arrangement with threats. Problems of capacity (that is, attempting marriage despite the presence of impediments) or problems with matrimonial form (the ceremonies of the wedding) also might render a marriage invalid. The annulment process attempts to discern whether there were any mitigating factors that compromised the mutual consent of the spouses to such an extent that the marriage was never valid.

A marriage bond is not dissolved when one or both spouses

commit adultery. Although divorce is not permitted in such a case, physical separation is permitted. Physical separation of bed and board may even be necessary for a limited or an indefinite time if one spouse poses grave mental or physical danger to the other (*CCC* 1649–50; *CCL* 1153).

Regardless of the reasons for separation, a gravely evil situation exists when one of the spouses begins to live with a third party or marries again without obtaining an annulment from the Church. Those who are married in the Church but who divorce and remarry civilly, for example, live in an objectively disordered or sinful situation. Therefore they cannot receive holy Communion as long as the situation persists.

CONCLUSION: BY THE GRACE OF GOD

Throughout sacred Scripture, God steadily reveals his lofty plan for marriage. The Lord instituted marriage from the beginning, and endowed it with three goods: children, fidelity, and indissolubility. Christ then raised marriage to the dignity of a sacrament. Christ fully reveals the pattern of mutual self-sacrificing love in his preaching and, above all, in his sacrifice on the cross. Through the sacrament of matrimony, Christian couples participate in the merits of Christ's sacrifice and in the relationship of eternal fidelity between Christ and his bride, the Church.

The Christian matrimonial bond is formed in the essential rite of the mutual consent of the Christian couple, who serve both as ministers and recipients of the sacrament. The invisible effects of the sacrament of matrimony include the establishment of the Christian conjugal bond, as well as the particular graces that consecrate and enable an individual to fulfill the vocations of spouse and parent. By the grace of Christ offered in this and other sacraments, Christian spouses can attain the heights of human love as perfected by the love of God.

DISCUSSION QUESTIONS

1. *What is unique about the institution of matrimony?*

2. *What constitutes the essential rite of the sacrament of matrimony?*

3. *What does it mean to "assist" at the sacrament of matrimony?*

4. *List the goods of marriage.*

5. *What is the difference between conjugal love and the conjugal act?*

ABBREVIATIONS AND SOURCES

CC: Pope Pius XI. "Encyclical on Christian Marriage" *Casti Connubii*. December 31, 1930.

CCC: *Catechism of the Catholic Church*. 1601–1666.

CCL: *Code of Canon Law*. Canons 1055–1165.

CT 24: Council of Trent, Session 24. The Doctrine of the Sacrament of Matrimony. November 11, 1563.

DV: Congregation for the Doctrine of the Faith. Instruction on Respect for Human Life in Its Origin and on the Dignity of Procreation: Replies to Certain Questions of the Day *Donum Vitae*. February 22, 1987. © 1987 Libreria Editrice Vaticana.

FC: Pope John Paul II. Apostolic Exhortation on the Role of the Christian Family in the Modern World *Familiaris Consortio*. November 22, 1981. © 1981 Libreria Editrice Vaticana.

GS: The Second Vatican Council. Pastoral Constitution on the Church in the Modern World *Gaudium et Spes*. December 7, 1965.

HV: Paul VI. Encyclical on the Regulation of Birth *Humanae Vitae*. July 25, 1968.

FOR FURTHER READING

Congregation for the Doctrine of the Faith. Concerning the Reception of Holy Communion by the Divorced and Remarried Members of the Faithful. September 14, 1994.

De Haro, Ramón García. *Marriage and the Family in the Documents of the Magisterium: A Course in the Theology of Marriage*, 2nd ed. Trans. William E. May. San Francisco: Ignatius Press, 1993.

Fastiggi, Robert. *What the Church Teaches about Sex: God's Plan for Happiness.* Huntington, IN: Our Sunday Visitor, 2008.

Peters, Edward N. *Annulments and the Catholic Church: Straight Answers to Tough Questions.* Rev. ed. West Chester, PA: Ascension Press, 2004.

Pontifical Council for the Family. Declaration on the Decrease of Fertility in the World. February 27, 1998.

Pontifical Council for the Family. Preparation for the Sacrament of Marriage. May 13, 1996.

Pontifical Council for the Family. *Vademecum* for Confessors Concerning Some Aspects of the Morality of Conjugal Life. February 12, 1997.

Rite of Marriage. In *The Rites of the Catholic Church*, vol. 1, pp. 717–758. 2nd edition. New York: Pueblo Publishing Company, 1992.

Conclusion

Christian Life and the Seven Sacraments

This book has been dedicated to a positive exposition of the seven sacraments, including the Church's doctrine and practice. The first chapter introduced key concepts that constitute the working vocabulary for studying Christian worship, including liturgy, sacrament, participation, rite, and Rite. Each of the seven chapters that followed explored the Church's belief in and practice of one of the seven sacraments: baptism, confirmation, the holy sacrifice of the Mass, penance, anointing of the sick, holy orders, and matrimony.

Each chapter demonstrated how a particular sacrament is "a visible sign of an invisible grace, instituted for our justification." That is, we discussed how our Lord instituted the sacrament, the elements of its essential rite (matter, form, minister, and recipient), and its invisible effect or grace. We also explored the importance of and the means for achieving full participation in each of the seven sacraments.

The preceding chapters were devoted to the Church's beautiful belief in the sacraments, not the crises or negative trends affecting participation in these sacraments. It would be naive, however, to deny or ignore such negative trends. Therefore we must address, before concluding, the widespread crisis in sacramental participation, which is afflicting the church throughout the world.

In many ways, the liturgical life of the Church appears to be in decline. The number of parents presenting infants for baptism has fallen dramatically. A surprisingly low percentage of Christians baptized in early childhood receive the sacrament of confirmation. Awareness of and belief in the Real Presence of Christ in the Eucharist are difficult to find, and very few people request priests to offer the sacrifice of the Mass for their intentions. Lines for the sacrament of penance are paltry in most churches. Too many Catholics die without receiving the sacrament of anointing of the sick. Many local churches suffer from a lack of vocations to the sacrament of holy orders. With fewer and fewer couples marrying, with divorce rates astronomically high, and with a growing percentage of children being born out of wedlock, marriage appears to be crumbling even within the Church.

This crisis in the sacraments reflects a larger crisis in Christian life as a whole. Our Lord summarized the Christian life with the Beatitudes (Matthew 5:1–12) and with his invitation, "Whoever wishes to come after me must deny himself, take up his cross, and follow me" (Mark 8:34). In the light of the Church's teaching on the divine sacrifice of the Mass, full and fruitful participation in the Eucharist entails taking on the mind of Christ as priest and victim, which means taking up one's cross. The Lord's exacting invitation to fully participate in his one sacrifice is at the heart of Christian and sacramental life. If we do not take up our crosses and wholeheartedly embrace the mission Christ entrusted to us through our baptism and confirmation, then we do not respond to our Lord's invitation, and the life of grace within us languishes.

There is a solution to the crisis in Christian life and the crisis in liturgical and sacramental participation. That solution is humble repentance and a wholehearted conversion toward the love and mercy that Christ offers to us in the holy sacraments. Humility must be at the heart of the disposition by which the faithful fruitfully participate in divine worship and the sacraments.

In this regard, a renewal of interest in and recourse to the sacrament of penance could lead to a revival of the grace offered to believers in the sacramental characters of their baptism and confirmation. In humility, those who have been blessed with the sacraments of matrimony and of holy orders will live out their vocations in the power and virtue of the Holy Spirit, strengthened by the special graces God gives in these sacraments. In humility, fruitful participation in the most holy sacrament of the Eucharist will support the Christian life of self-sacrificing charity in union with Christ's sacrifice on Calvary. In humility and fortified by the grace of the sacraments, the faithful will fulfill their charge to evangelize the world, participating in the mission of our Lord Jesus Christ. As the Second Vatican Council teaches, the Church faithfully guards Christ's "precepts of charity, humility and self-sacrifice," and "receives the mission to proclaim and to spread among all peoples the Kingdom of Christ and of God and to be, on earth, the initial budding forth of that kingdom" (LG 5). Through the seven sacraments of the new law, our Lord imparts this mission to the faithful and offers us the grace to fulfill it.

9 780764 818455